ALSO BY DENISE BATTEES:

Talking To Heaven, The Simple Basics

(Available only through her web site:
www.deniseroot.com)

Beyond Belief

A Medium's Amazing Journey
through Near-Death Experiences,
Channeling Her Guides, and a Walk-In

DENISE BATTEES

BALBOA.
PRESS

A DIVISION OF HAY HOUSE

Balboa Press books may be ordered through booksellers or by contacting:

Balboa Press
A Division of Hay House
1663 Liberty Drive
Bloomington, IN 47403
www.balboapress.com
1 (877) 407-4847

Because of the dynamic nature of the Internet, any web addresses or links contained in this book may have changed since publication and may no longer be valid. The views expressed in this work are solely those of the author and do not necessarily reflect the views of the publisher, and the publisher hereby disclaims any responsibility for them.

The author of this book does not dispense medical advice or prescribe the use of any technique as a form of treatment for physical, emotional, or medical problems without the advice of a physician, either directly or indirectly. The intent of the author is only to offer information of a general nature to help you in your quest for emotional and spiritual well-being. In the event you use any of the information in this book for yourself, which is your constitutional right, the author and the publisher assume no responsibility for your actions.

Any people depicted in stock imagery provided by Thinkstock are models, and such images are being used for illustrative purposes only.
Certain stock imagery © Thinkstock.

Printed in the United States of America.

ISBN: 978-1-4525-8804-9 (sc)
ISBN: 978-1-4525-8805-6 (e)

Balboa Press rev. date: 12/12/2013

To God,
my loving Spirit Guides and Loved ones
in Heaven for their inspiration and guidance.

Contents

Preface

I AM JUST a plain and simple girl who has been on an interesting journey called life. However, there is nothing normal about my life or my journey through it. Since I was a small girl, I have always had invisible friends. I could not see them, but somehow I knew they were there because I could feel them. I feared them at first, thinking they were the boogie man, (as my brothers called them). No wonder I feared them so much, I was taught to fear from a small age. Over the years these invisible friends have always been with me, guiding me through danger and turmoil, and loving me when I felt so alone and unloved. It was years before I learned that my invisible friends were actually called "Spirit Guides" and that they were sent by God to guide me through this life.

Over the years, they became such a part of me that I learned to trust them with all of my being. They have never left me. They were with me through all my near death experiences, guiding my way to the other side and back. They were with me during my many visits to Heaven and my walk in experiences and they continue to guide me to the other side when God calls on me. I have never considered myself to be special. Quite the opposite. I always felt weird and out of place in this world, almost like I didn't belong. For years I kept my guides to myself for fear of being judged or ridiculed, but with the help of my Spirit Guides, I have learned to overcome my fears and move forward with their guidance.

After years of meditation and working with my guides on a daily basis. I have learned to hear them and see them as well as feel them. I continue to grow stronger every day and through my Spirit Guides encouragement, I overcame my shyness and started my business; "Messages From Heaven" to help even more people overcome their fear of death and to give them validations that their loved ones on the other side are safe and at peace. More importantly, that death is not final, but merely another form of living. Today, I am a well know Psychic Medium and I continue to channel my loving guides and Jesus, to teach others the truth about the place called Heaven.

Guided by my loving Spirit Guides to educate others, I am encouraged to tell you my story.

This is a true account of my personal journey and all that I have experienced along the way. I hope that my story will inspire you in some way.

In The Beginning

M Y MEMORIES BEGIN as small young girl, at the age of three was twirling endlessly on an old rusty bar in the front yard of her home. Feeling safe, loved and without a care in the world. The bar was an old piece of pipe sticking up from the ground that had been left there from another tenant that once occupied the home. It's funny how I could find the simplest things to occupy my time. Even though I had brothers and a sister, I preferred to play alone so I could use my imagination without getting picked on.

Twirling on that rusty bar made me feel like I was flying. I would twirl faster and faster until I made myself dizzy. After hours of twirling I would go into the house and give my grandmother a hug. My grandmother lived with us and watched over us while my parents worked. Grandma always had an apron on while she was cleaning the house and cooking the meals for the family. I loved the apron strings that hung down and would often grab them and hold on tight. It gave me a sense of security and I knew she was only an apron string away. I loved grandma with all my heart and had to be with her where ever she went. When grandma was in the kitchen cooking, I was right beside her snapping green beans or throwing the potato peels in the garbage, whatever I could do to help her.

My eyes were wide as I asked my grandmother a million questions, like a thirsty sponge soaking up all the information. The house would fill with the aroma of home cooked meals and fresh baked goods. I especially loved grandma's homemade cookies because I got to help stir and nibble the cookie dough. Peanut butter cookies were my favorite. When the day was coming to a close and the chores were done, I would race upstairs for my bath and then jump into the big bed that grandma and I shared. Grandma would always talk to me until I fell asleep. I always slept deeply knowing that grandma was only a reach away.

My mother worked two jobs during the day and didn't get home until we were in bed most of the time. My dad was a truck driver and was on the road all week long. We would all look forward to him coming home on the weekends. I remember all of us kids running to the door when he got home to catch up on our much needed hugs and kisses. I was the youngest of four children, and dad always called me his baby girl.

The weekends were always too short and before we knew it dad was gone again. Even though I missed my dad very much, I still had my grandma with me. When

I was four we moved to a different house and I remember starting kindergarten that year. My mom had taken me to meet my teacher and see my classroom. I was excited to see all the toys in the room and my teacher seemed nice. I got home and told grandma that even though I was excited for school, I was scared and wanted to stay home with her. Grandma just smiled and said I was a big girl and that my brothers and sister would walk me to and from school. She told me to wait outside the school until my brothers came for me.

Everything was going as scheduled and everyday my brothers would meet me by the doors and walk me home. I was always so anxious to get home to grandma and share my day. The weekends would come and go and I still looked forward to my dad coming home and spending time with me. You would think that I had the perfect life, but that was farthest from the truth.

My dad came home on the weekend and I remember he and my mother having a bad argument. The next thing I knew Dad was gone and my mother had filed for divorce. Grandma kept consoling me and telling me it would be alright, but something inside me changed that day. I had a hole in my heart that ached for my dad. Grandma told me to pray every night and ask God to bring daddy back. Night after night I prayed for God to bring daddy back. Months passed and the hole in my heart grew bigger, but I still had grandma to hold me and love me. I grew even closer to my grandmother after that.

Life Changing Events

FIRST NEAR DEATH experience:

At the young age of four, just a few short months after my dad left our home; I got out of school and was standing by the doors just as I had done many times before. My older siblings were supposed to get me and walk me home safely, but that day I knew my grandma was baking cookies and I couldn't wait to get home to help her. My brothers were taking too long to get me so I ran ahead. I knew the way home and I was sure I could do it alone. I ran the first two blocks, crossing at the intersections with the help of the crossing guards and when I got to the third street, there was no crossing guard because there was a traffic light. I knew to wait for the light and to look both ways, but the light seemed to be stuck on red and it was taking too long. I was in a hurry and I didn't want to wait because I wanted to see my grandma, so I ran as fast as I could across the street.

The road was four lanes wide; I remember the loud horns honking and the sound of breaks squealing. I don't know how I made it across the first three lanes, but when I got to the fourth lane I remember being slammed to the ground. Everything went dark and it felt like everything was spinning around me. As though I was caught in a tornado spinning endlessly. I could hear the roaring of an engine running above me, and the ground I was laying on was vibrating from the engine. Then I saw a beautiful bright light coming toward me. The light seemed to wrap me in a blanket of comfort, but it was so bright that I couldn't open my eyes; I just kept spinning in circles. I remember my head hurt from hitting the pavement. The next thing I remember is waking up on the ground with a police man talking to me and telling me everything would be alright. The policeman had placed his hat under my head for a cushion, and I remember everyone looking down at me lying on the ground. I could hear everyone talking to me, but the voices were muffled. The policeman told me to lay still and not move. I became dizzy again and seemed to pass out.

The next conscious moment was waking up to the sound of loud sirens. I remember being in the ambulance and I could hear people talking to me. I was feeling all the bumps in the road and I remember a man looking down at me and trying to comfort me, telling me it was going to be okay. I had an oxygen mask on my face and tubes were going everywhere. Even though this stranger was nice to me, I still felt very afraid. I didn't know him or where he was taking me and I had to get home to my grandma because she would be worried. I tried to get up but then I realized I was strapped down and couldn't move. I blacked out again.

My next conscious memory was waking up in a hospital bed. I heard voices talking again. This time it was the doctor talking to my mother. I had a heavy cotton wrap on my head and a cast on my arm and I remember my head was hurting bad. My mother said I was run over by a dump truck just a foot from the curb. She told me that I had been in a deep sleep for days and they were glad to see me finally wake up. I had a severe concussion, a broken arm and several cuts to my face and head. They were picking the gravel out my head for days. The police officer told my mother that I was just one inch away from getting my head crushed by the dual rear wheels on the dump truck. My head injuries were so severe, the doctors didn't know how I survived that accident. That was my first brush with death.

When I was seven years old my mother started dating a new man and we had moved in with him. It was a large old two story house with five bedrooms. My grandma's bedroom was down stairs off the dining room and I was told that I could not sleep with grandma anymore because I was getting too big. I had the small bedroom at the top of the stairs and my three brothers would all share the large bedroom behind me. My sister got the other small bedroom just off the boy's room. I was not used to sleeping without grandma and I had a hard time sleeping by myself. I had developed a fear of the dark, and that house was old and full of creaks and strange noises. I always felt like someone was in the room watching me, but when I looked around the room all I could see was shadows cast on the wall from the light coming through the small window in my room. I ran to my brother's bedroom and told them that someone was watching me. They laughed at me and said it was the boogie man under my bed. That only added to the fear of being separated from my grandmother's side.

I remember being terrified to go to bed at night in my own little room. Every night I would feel the presence of someone watching me, yet when I looked around, no one was there. The trees moving outside my window, swaying in the wind, continued to cast the shadows on my wall. It only scared me more and all I could do was shut my eyes tight and not look at the shadows. I knew that I could not go to my brothers because they would continue to pick on me. I was trying to be brave but the fear inside me was strong. I came downstairs and tried to tell my mother that I was scared to sleep alone, but she just got mad at me and thought it was just an excuse to return to my grandma's bed and forbid it. Once again, I was sent to my little room alone. I was never afraid when I slept with grandma because she was always right there beside me and now I had that comfort taken away.

The next day after school, I raced home to talk to grandma before everyone else got there. I told her about the strangers and my fears and she just smiled and hugged me. She told me that she too had felt a presence in the room all the time, and she told me not to fear them because they would not hurt me. I asked her who they were and all she would say is that they were watching over me and someday when I was older she would explain.

A few months later I got very sick. I was burning up with fever and I had a hard time swallowing. My grandmother had made me some hot tea with honey and asked made me drink it. She put some medicine on a towel and wrapped it around my neck. She was constantly taking my temperature and telling my mother that she was getting concerned. This went on for days. Grandma was letting me sleep with her so she could watch over me during my sickness. When I felt better and my fever finally broke my mother made me return to my own bedroom. Once again, the fears came back and I could feel the presence of someone in my room. I just closed my eyes and remembered grandma telling me that they would not hurt me. Grandma bought a small night light and plugged it in my room and that seemed to bring some comfort to me. Over the years, I continued to feel my invisible friends with me but somehow I became used to them and I did not fear them anymore.

Second near death experience:

At the age of seven, I remember it being a really hot day, and all of us kids were restless from the heat. My oldest brother had convinced my mom to let us go swimming at the local river. We found a place that was fairly shallow because I did not know how to swim. The river water was always cold but it was a welcomed shock to our overheated bodies. We were all having fun running down the bank of the river and jumping in. My brothers kept dunking me and I didn't like it. I always choked when I got water up my nose, so I decided to go farther down the bank so they could not dunk me. I ran down the river bank and jumped in just like I had done many times before, but this time something went wrong. I remember jumping in and going down and down. I could not touch the bottom and I did not know how to swim. I had hit a drop off and the strong currents of the river were sucking me under. My eyes were open and the water was very black and murky. I remember holding my breath and struggling to feel ground beneath my feet. As much as I hated feeling the slimy seaweed on my feet, I would have welcomed that. I was getting more and more tired, struggling to get to the top of the water, and couldn't hold my breath anymore. My body went limp and I seemed to be floating away in the currents.

Then once again I felt that familiar presence of my invisible friends and it comforted me. I remember seeing a beautiful white light coming through the water toward me and surrounding me once again. As if an angel was wrapping me in her wings. I wasn't feeling afraid anymore. I felt very comforted by the light and it helped me to forget where I was and what was happening to me, then I lost consciousness.

The next memory was lying on the banks of the river hearing voices calling my name and telling me to wake up. As I was waking up I remember choking on water and struggling to get a breath. When I opened my eyes I saw my brother's friend, who had joined us that day and was the best swimmer among us. He had jumped in and pulled me out. I don't know how long I was under the water or what happened to me after I blacked out. I only remember that I wasn't alone and that my invisible friends were there with me. That was my second brush with death.

A few months later while my mom was at work, the man that lived with us loaded us in the car and took us fishing. It was a gravel pit of some sort with a bridge beside it. There were huge piles of rocks and sand. He said it was one of his favorite spots to fish. It was the same river that I had almost drowned in earlier, just farther down the river. We were all running around playing on the sand piles and my brothers were chasing me with a bug. I remember screaming and running to the man to make my brothers stop. To my surprise, he grabbed me by the back of the shirt and held me out over the water, dangling me off the bridge and telling me if I didn't stop screaming and scaring the fish he was going to drop me.

I was terrified and was kicking and screaming for fear he would drop me into the river. I kicked so hard that I kicked one of my shoes off and watched as it fell all the way to the river below. When I got home he told my mother and I got punished for losing one of my school shoes. I disliked that man from that day forward, and I felt as though my invisible friends were warning me to stay away from him.

Later that summer I remember packing to move to yet another house. I was glad to leave that creaky old house with the spooky shadows. But what I did not know, was that this time my grandma would not be coming with us to the new house. We were moving to a smaller house that only had three bedrooms and there was no room for grandma. My grandmother went to live with her sister in a far away town and we were told that we could visit her. Even though grandma would be leaving, the move brought some excitement when I learned that this time I would be sharing a bedroom with my sister. I no longer had the fear of being alone. Even though my sister was four years older than me and picked on me a lot, I was happy to have her close. The room we shared was fairly small so my mother had purchased bunk beds for us. I had the top bunk and she took the bottom. There was a sense of security knowing she was just below me.

Somehow I felt a connection to this house. It felt very familiar to me and I was later told that it was the same house my dad had bought for my mother when she was pregnant for me. They were living in that home when I born and years later they lost the house. My mother said she was surprised to find that it was back up for sale and she didn't hesitate to grab it. Knowing the story behind the house somehow made me feel closer to my dad. Our first night in the new house was exciting but yet strange. Trying to get used to the new setting and a feel of the house. We had taken all day to get our room in order and get all our things put away. As I laid there looking around, once again I felt that feeling of someone in the room watching me. I looked around and saw nothing, but I was comforted in knowing that my invisible friends had followed us in the move.

The new house brought a lot of changes. My mother had gotten a new job working second shift at a factory. He got a new job as well and was working day shift. We were in school during the day and when we got home, mom was already gone to work and he would be there to watch us. We had a large yard so they bought us a round pool that set on the ground and he put it up for us. It was hot that day and we were anxious to get in. I still did not know how to swim and I remember looking at the pool with fear that I would not be able to stand up in it. All the other kids were jumping in and I just stood on the ground watching them. He came out and asked why I was not in the pool. I told him I was afraid because I still did not know how to swim. He grabbed me by the back of the shirt and threw me in the pool. He stood there laughing at me while I was thrashing and kicking, choking on water and trying to touch the bottom. I remember my oldest brother coming to aid me, helping me to the side of the pool where I could hold on. Everyday after that, my brothers worked with me in the pool until I learned how to dog paddle. Once again I did not like that man.

I remember one weekend we were going on a road trip to see grandma. It was a long two hour drive to get there and I was so excited to see her. I remember pulling up to an old building with several apartments. Grandma met us at the door with hugs and kisses and took us upstairs to her apartment. She showed us around her new place and introduced us to her sister that lived in the apartment across the hall. We spent the day running back and forth between apartments. When it was time to go I had a strange feeling of sadness come over me. I felt as though it would be a long time before I would see her again. That feeling held true.

Grandma's passing:

I remember my mother getting letters from grandma and she would always read them to us. One day the letter from grandma brought some bad news. Grandma had hurt her hip and she had to be in the hospital for awhile. Mom told us that grandma was moving back to town, but that she would have to stay in a nursing home to take care of her because she was sick. I was happy that she would be closer and that we could see her more often. I remember our first visit to see grandma. We walked down a long hall with a lot of rooms. Grandma's room was at the end of the hall, I ran to her and asked if she was okay. She smiled and assured me she was fine. We hugged and kissed and talked about how I was doing. Every time we would visit grandma we always stopped at the D.Q to pickup her favorite pineapple shake. I remember visiting her for several weekends and always looked forward to it.

On one of our visits I remember her and mom having a serious talk. They sent me to the hallway so they could have some privacy, but I still heard some of their conversation. I remember grandma begging my mother to promise her that she would never marry the man we were living with. She told my mother that she saw evil in him and said if my mother married him it would affect us kids in a bad way. After a long talk, my mother finally promised not to marry him.

Then one night it was really late and I had fallen asleep on the couch. I woke up with the sound of my mother getting home from work. She was tired and getting ready to go to bed when the phone rang. It was the nursing home where grandma was staying; they called to tell my mom that grandma was getting bad and that she needed to come now. My mother sat back down and must have fallen asleep in the chair because a couple hours later the phone rang again and woke me up. This time they told my mom that Grandma was gone. I remember mom crying and feeling bad that she didn't go the first time they called. Was there something that my grandma wanted to tell her? She felt bad that she didn't get a chance to say goodbye. That memory would haunt my mother for years to come.

I was only nine when my precious grandmother passed away. I was told that it was her time to go to Heaven. I remember crying frantically and asking why I couldn't go with her. It felt like someone had ripped the heart from my chest and I could not breathe. All I knew was that I went everywhere with my grandma and I didn't understand why she left without me. A few days later my mother loaded all us kids in the car and she told us were going to say goodbye to Grandma. It was a long drive and when we got there, I remember rushing in to see her.

As I entered the big room, I remember going up to the casket where my Grandma was sleeping. I tried to talk to her but she did not wake up. I reached for her hand and squeezed it just like I always did when I needed to be comforted. I was begging her to wake up. I told her I was upset with her because she left without me. My mother stepped in at that time and told me that Grandma would never wake up and that we had to say goodbye. I was so upset and I wanted to crawl in that box and go with her. I remember screaming and crying frantically. I grabbed my grandma's dress and refused to let go. My mother was pulling on me and telling me to let go. All I knew was that I had to hold on or I would lose her forever. A man came up to my mother and told her to take me outside and calm me down. The next thing I remember is driving to a place and watching Grandma being lowered into the ground. Again I was frantic. She can't breathe in that box I said, don't put dirt on my grandma. Once again, I wanted to go with her. I remember crying all the way home and my mother was reprimanding me for being naughty. I felt like my world was crashing. When my dad left I was devastated, and now Grandma had left me too. The only two people in the world that loved me were gone and I didn't know how to bring them back. I had an enormous feeling of dread and abandonment. I felt like something inside me had died too.

Finding God

EVEN THOUGH MY mother made a promise to my grandma that she would never marry the man we lived with, she married him seven short months after my grandmother's passing and my life was never the same. I lived in constant fear from that day forward.

On my 10th birthday, my dad came to see me. Dad was not allowed in the house so he waited out by the curb next to his car. My mother sent me outside to see him. I was overjoyed it had been years since I had seen him. He had bought me a birthday cake and a gift. I remember standing out there for hours with my dad. The other kids came out to see him too. We had to cut the cake with my dad's jack knife and eat it with our fingers, because dad had forgotten to bring paper plates. He told us kids that he was living in Florida now and would only get to see us when he was in town. But that he loved and missed us very much. He asked my mom if it would be okay for his mother and sister to come and visit us kids. Mom accepted, but again telling him they were not allowed in her home. They would have to call ahead and wait out on the curb just like he had done. Dad's visit came to an end and we had to say goodbye and once again my heart broke.

A few weeks later my mom got us all dressed up and told us that our Aunt and other grandma was coming to visit. I did not have a strong bond with this grandma because I hadn't seen her that much. I remember her always having butterscotch candies when she visited and it was always a treat for us kids. My grandmother and aunt pulled up by the curb and once again, my mother filed us out the door. We gave our hugs and got into the car and they took us to a nice restaurant for lunch. I remember mom telling us to be on our best behavior during our visit. When the food got to our table, grandma asked us not to eat until we blessed the food and then I remembered dad's stories about his mother. This grandma was a Minister, and she is the one that taught me all about God and Jesus.

During her visit I asked her questions about God and she was more than willing to tell me about him. She encouraged us to go to church and learn more about God and told us how important it was to be saved in the name of Jesus. She told us to love Jesus and he would watch over us and protect us. At that moment it made me think of my invisible friends. I told her about them and that they did not talk to me but I could feel them. I told her that my other grandma said not to fear them and that she was going to tell me who they were when I got older, but she went to Heaven before she could tell me. I didn't understand why I could feel them and no one else could. I didn't want to be different and everyone was picking on me because of it. My grandma just hugged me and said "My child, God has given you a special gift and someday he will call on you to help others. Do not fear them because they are here to help you". She said to just pray and talk to God and he would teach me.

The next week, the strangest thing happened. A man knocked at the door and said he was from a nearby church. He told us that they would be bringing a bus past our house every Sunday and was looking for children to come to Sunday school. My sister and I jumped at the chance, and with a lot of begging, mom finally gave her permission. So every Sunday we would put our dresses on and wait for the bus.

We learned so much about God and Angels. My sister and I were saved at that church and were given a beautiful new bible. A few weeks later our Sunday school teacher came to us and asked if we would like to be baptized for Jesus. I remember how important that was for my other grandma, so we signed up. The next Sunday during church I was baptized. I wore the long white robe that was given to me by the minister and I remember stepping down into the tank. The water was warm and comforting. The minister knew I was afraid of water so he placed his folded handkerchief over my nose and mouth and was very careful not to get water up my nose during the dunk. Just before he dunked me I could feel the presence of my invisible friends with me. When I was in the water a familiar rush came over me and I felt peaceful. I remember people clapping and singing songs as he was pulling me from the water. I felt something change in me that day, something good happened. I was eleven years old when I was baptized in the name of Jesus, I was God's child now and I knew he would protect me and never leave me. My sister and I continued to go to church until the bus stopped coming for us.

I went thru hell for the next several years. I really disliked my step dad and feared him a lot. I felt so uneasy around him and was unhappy at home so I stayed away as much as I could. I was going to school functions, babysitting and staying at my friend's houses.

When I was fifteen, my brother introduced me to a friend of his. He was a year older than me and he had his license and a pickup truck and he came over every day. We would all pile in his truck and leave for the day. We would go swimming at the local lake or go to the park, anything to get us out of the house. I talked to my mom about it and she seemed to like him and encouraged me to keep seeing this boy. I continued to see him throughout the next school year. He lived a block away and every morning I would walk over to his house to meet him, then we would walk to school together. My heart grew fond of him and when I was with him he made me feel safe. His parents were very kind to me and we became very close.

In August of 1977 just a few days after his 18th birthday we said our vows before God.

The first few years were ruff but we were happy and made it through. The following years of my marriage were not so smooth. I had lost four babies to miscarriage and finally gave birth to a beautiful daughter. A couple years later I could feel my husband growing distant. We had grown apart and I was on an emotional roller coaster. I was so stressed out that I became really sick. When my daughter was two years old, my husband's best friend Andy stopped by. He and my husband grew up together and were like brothers, but when I met my husband it was like a tug of war. We both wanted to be with him and there were bad feelings, so Andy backed away to give me more time with him. He wouldn't even come to our wedding when we got married. We had not seen him in four years. He had grown up a lot. He was clean cut, well dressed and had just finished college. We caught up on old times and we became close friends again. Andy came for several visits over the years and we would do everything together. We became like the three musketeers. As we got closer I trusted Andy enough to tell him that I had been having trouble in our marriage. I loved my husband so I stayed with him, but I didn't know how much more I could take. Andy already knew that we were having trouble because my husband had confided in him about everything and he promised me that he was going to talk with him about it when he got back. He told me he was leaving town the next day for business, but he promised to have that talk when he returned in a couple days. I told him to drive careful and I watched him back out of the driveway.

I counted the hours until Andy's return. I went to bed that night knowing he would be back the next day. I could only pray that he would convince my husband to change.

I was sound asleep when the phone rang at 2:00 am. I will never forget the voice on the other end of the phone. It was Andy's dad calling to tell me that there was an accident. He said that Andy was driving back to his hotel that night and had hit some loose sand on the road causing his car to go into a skid and crash. My heart sank and I felt a heavy feeling of dread. I asked if he was okay and his father told me that Andy was killed instantly. I burst into tears and screamed NO! Three days later we went to the funeral. As I walked up to the casket, I had flash backs of my grandmother's funeral. I felt so alone. I loved him so much and I never got to tell him that.

When my daughter was four years old I found myself pregnant again. I looked at it in a positive way. My husband had always wanted a son and maybe this was a way of bringing us closer again. The day I went into labor for my son, he drove me to the hospital and stayed with me until I delivered the baby. While I was still in recovery, he went home to get some sleep. Shortly after he left the nurse came in to get the name of the baby. We planned to name him after his father, and Andy was to be the middle name in honor of our friend who had passed away. But when I looked into my son's tiny little face, I heard a voice whisper the name Andy, so I changed his name around giving him Andy's name first and his father's middle name.

I brought my son home from the hospital and grew to love him more every day. My husband was okay with me changing his name around. He said that he wanted to honor his best friend too. As I watched my son grow, it warmed my heart to know that he was named after someone dear to my heart. It also helped to remind me of Andy and how much he meant to me. We had both agreed that my son would to be my last child. I had carried six babies in my womb and four of them were in Heaven.

Over the years my husband and I continued to have marital problems. My husband did not want to be with me anymore and every time he left the house I would get a bad feeling in the pit of my stomach. One day he came home and I confronted him and I told him I could not take it anymore and that I was filing for divorce. When my son turned six the divorce was final.

Two years later my ex husband started coming around again. He had made a lot of changes to his life and had gone through counseling. He was returning to the man I married years ago. He wanted another chance and after being divorced for two years I had become lonely so I agreed to start dating him again. After about a year I agreed to let him move back in. The first few years were good and I began to fall in love again.

The Sickness

A T THE AGE of 39, I remember getting very sick and weak. My body was in constant pain and it was years of endless testing before I would finally get a diagnoses of Lupus. I struggled with the disease for four years and it seemed to be getting worse. I was in and out of hospitals due to the reactions to all the drugs I was taking and I could not take them anymore. The specialist told me that if I did not take the medicine the Lupus would take my life. My family doctor told me that if I continued to take the medicine, the side effects would kill me. I was so afraid. I didn't have a choice. The doctors agreed to send me to Ann Arbor for testing and to see if there was a new experimental drug I could try. I was worried that I would not be able to take any more medicines. So I began getting my will in order. After a lot of praying, I decided to go to my grandmother's grave. I knew she was close to God and if anyone could help it would be her. I drove for 3 hours to get to her resting place. I pulled up beside her grave and when I got out of the car every hair on my body stood up. This was the first time I had been there since her passing. I knelt down beside her and began to cry and pray. I asked her to talk to God and put in a good word for me. I felt like I was at the end of the road and did not know what to do. Being with her brought me some comfort that day.

Days later I went to Ann Arbor and went thru two days of rigorous testing, and then I was sent home to wait. It took three weeks to get the test results and when the phone rang that day it brought good news. The tests showed that the Lupus was in remission. A feeling of overwhelming gratitude came over me and I just knew that my grandmother helped my prayers to be heard. My life was back on track and all the symptoms from the disease had gone away.

During my four years of sickness, I started getting that feeling in the pit of my stomach again. My ex husband had grown tired of me being sick all the time and the love between us was gone. We were just staying together for the kids.

After my lupus went into remission I felt good for a couple years, but then something else happened. Walking four miles every day was part of my routine. I walked every night after work and I was walking about a mile from the house when all of the sudden my legs collapsed beneath me and I fell to the ground. I remember lying by the side of the road feeling embarrassed and was struggling to get to my feet. I realized that I could not feel anything from the waist down and my legs were not working. I immediately began to pray to God, asking him to give me the strength to get to my feet. "Please dear God, don't leave me here on the side of the road".

I was embarrassed that someone would see me. I just kept praying and praying. Then all of the sudden I felt strength come into my legs and I struggled to my feet. I turned around and walked straight home to tell my ex what had happened. The next day I went to the doctor for tests and the MRI had revealed four masses in my brain. The doctor explained the he believed the masses were tumors. He needed to do surgery to see what kind of cancer we were dealing with. He explained that one of the tumors was so deep in my brain that for him to go that deep may result in memory loss, paralysis or even death. He gave me a 50/50 chance of even waking up from the surgery. I went home and began praying to God. My ex husband was clear that he did not want any part of the surgery he refused to even go to the hospital the day of surgery, even though my chances of recovery was slim. But after many harsh words from my brothers, he agreed to only stay till the surgery was over.

A couple days later I went to the hospital for surgery. They came into the room and shaved my head. They took me to surgery and performed the first phase of screwing the heavy cage to my head. I woke up in recovery and had a head ache from hell. The cage was really heavy and I remember it weighing down on my neck. They placed a towel over the cage and wheeled me to CT. They had to get a picture of where the masses were located on the markings on the cage. That gave them an idea of where to drill. Then back to the holding room until the next surgery. While I was waiting for my second surgery they allowed my family to come in one last time. I cried as my children hugged me. I had a strong feeling inside me that this would be my final goodbye. I tried to smile and not show my fear as I told them that no matter what happened, to remember how much I loved them. Then we said our final goodbyes.

They came and wheeled me down the hall to the second surgery. I remember them placing me on the table and strapping me down. They lifted my head and locked me down into the machine that would drill. I had a strong feeling of dread come over me and the fear filled my body. All I could think of was my children. As the surgeon entered the room the fear welled up inside me and I began praying. I remember looking up at the bright surgical light above me and at that moment, the beautiful face of Jesus appeared to me. I stared into his loving face and an incredible feeling of peace came over me. The feeling of fear left my body and I felt a single tear run down my face as they put me under.

The surgery began and within moments things started to go wrong. The cage that they had screwed to my head had a door on the front of it. The door was an access to put my respirator tube in, but the cage was broken and the door would not open. I was already under and they had moments to get me on the respirator. They shoved a needle into my throat to relax my esophagus and then shoved the respirator between the bars of the cage sideways into my throat. When they put me under, my eyes were still fixed on the face of Jesus and were wide open during surgery, so they had to put gel in my eyes to keep them from drying out during surgery. At some point in the surgery my heart stopped, causing me to flat line. I was told that there were several attempts made to revive me and they didn't know if I was coming back. They did not tell me how long I was flat lined and I have no memory of what took place during that time.

I woke up nine hours later in intensive care. When I opened my eyes I had no memory of the surgery at all. I felt no pain and I had so much energy I felt as if I was going to burst. I spent the night in ICU and was moved to my room in the morning. When I got to my room I remember feeling very strange and I got up and went into the bathroom. When I looked in the mirror it was if a stranger was looking back at me. I did not feel like myself. My eyes were glazed over and still filled with the gel. My head was wrapped with thick white gauze and one of my eyes seemed to be crooked. When I came out of the bathroom my doctor was waiting and he told me what had happened. He said that when they put me under my eyes were wide open. I remembered seeing the face of Jesus and I did not want to take my eyes off him. He then sat me down and told me that there were complications during surgery and explained what happened. He told me that when they tried to get a piece of the mass to sample it, the needle kept bouncing off of it. He had to go deeper and when he finally did penetrate it, it crumbled like an empty egg shell. He told me that it definitely was not cancer and he had never seen anything like it, so they had sent it out to be tested.

My ex husband only stayed until the doctor came out to update the family and then he was gone. He said he needed some time away, so he retreated to our cabin up north. The day I was released I had to call my dad to bring me home. I felt like my prayers were answered. It was not cancer and the fear of dying left me. When I walked into my house, it felt very strange to me. It felt like it was the first time I had ever seen the house. I had lived in this house for fifteen years and I knew every inch of it, but somehow everything felt different. I can't explain it. There was a cold feeling about it. I could not feel any love there.

The Opening

WEEKS LATER I got the call from the hospital. They had sent my biopsy sample all the way to Mayo to be identified. It was scar tissue caused from Multiple Sclerosis. Apparently I had the disease long enough to do that kind of damage. Once again I had a disease, but this one did not bring a death sentence.

The days passed and somehow everything still felt strange to me. Something was not right. The brain surgery I just went through had changed me somehow. Ever since I got home from the hospital I felt different. I started to feel the presence of my imaginary friends again, but this time the feeling had grown stronger. Much stronger! I knew there were spirits in the room with me. I felt them so strong that I could count how many were there. The multiple spirits had made me feel uneasy. I was not used to so many of them. I kept praying to God to cast them out. The more I prayed, the more spirits I felt in the room. I feared it so much that I could not eat or sleep. I was missing a lot of time at work and had lost over 40 pounds. There were so many spirits that I had a panic attacks. I felt anxious and could not breathe. I ran outside to get away from them and remember praying for God's light and protection.

Then I heard a voice come out of nowhere and said "I am God's light"! I realized then that every time I asked for God's protection he would send more spirits to protect me. That's why there were so many of them. I asked, "how do I know if they are good or bad" and the voice said "You will know the difference, put your faith in the Lord and you shall be protected".

Later that night, I was lying on my bed crying about the lack of love and the emptiness I was feeling. I prayed to God for answers and as I laid there staring at the ceiling it made a very loud cracking noise, a vision flashed of the ceiling cracking open and at that instant I saw the hand of God come down as if he were reaching for me. The crack was so loud it made me jump. Then I heard a gentle loving voice say: "Be still my child, I have given you a gift and now it is the time I call upon you to use it."

I remember talking to my grandmother when I was a young girl and I asked her why I was different. Why was I able to feel things that others could not? She replied; "God has given you a special gift and someday he will call upon you to use it." I knew God was calling on me now, but how was I supposed to use it? What do I need to do? Grandma passed away before she could explain it to me.

I was off work for awhile after surgery and to take my mind off the spirit presence around me I turned the television on. There was a new show on and it was the first time I had ever seen it. It was interesting to me and I was drawn to it for some strange reason. The man on TV was communicating with the souls that passed over. I remember sitting on the edge of my chair absorbing everything he was saying. It was as if a light bulb was going off in me. I kept thinking I can do that too! I watched that show every day while I was off work. I could not get enough of it. I just kept thinking that my grandma was in Heaven and I needed to find her. But how do I look for her? How can I talk to her? A feeling of thirst came over me. I thirst for knowledge. I jumped in the car and drove to the library. I ran to the shelves searching for every book I could get my hands on. I took out all the books the library would allow at a time. When I finished them I would go back for more. I was a thirsty sponge, soaking up all the knowledge I could get. Was this what God had called me to do? The feeling inside me was so strong I could not fight it.

Weeks went by and you could not pull me away from the library. Then I found a book that seemed to speak to me. There was a chapter on how to meditate, and another chapter on how to call on a loved one. The book was easy to understand, giving me step by step instructions. So I began to meditate. Doing everything it instructed me to do. I lit a candle and went to my bedroom away from everyone. I took some deep breaths and envisioned surrounding myself with Gods holy light. I grounded myself and began my journey into meditation. Night after night I would meditate hoping to hear from my grandmother. Then on the fifth night it happened. I started my meditation as I always did, but this time I focused on my grandmother's face in my mind. I thought about all the love I had for her until my heart swelled then I started calling to her. The room began to get cold and I felt a whirling around me. My heart started to beat harder and suddenly I could feel her loving presence. I just knew she was there with me. I can't explain it, I just knew! I sat there in my chair absorbing her love and sobbing from my emotions. She did not speak she just stood beside me and let me feel her energy. I remember asking her if she was proud of me and in my mind I saw her smile. That was it! I knew that this worked and I knew I had to learn more. I had waited years to see my grandmother again and I was not going to stop now. Something inside me was driving me to learn more.

I continued to meditate every day, and I asked God to guide my meditations. Weeks passed and the cold feeling would always come during meditations and the feeling of someone with me got stronger. One night my daughter and I were sitting on the couch talking. It was late and everyone had gone to bed except the two of us. My granddaughter had left a toy out on the floor. It was a pole that you stack the round plastic rings on, stacking them from big to small. This one would light up and chime as you slid the rings on it. There was nothing around it to cause it to go off, but all of the sudden it just lit up. The lights started flashing and it began to chime. Our feet were up on the couch and there was no vibration on the floor to make it do that. My daughter and I just looked at each other in disbelief. Then I felt a presence in the room and the toy started to flash and chime again. I asked who was doing that and I heard a voice say "Andy". It was our best friend Andy who was killed in a car crash 16 years earlier. I had thought about him all the time. I asked him if he knew that I had named my son after him and he replied; "I am the one who whispered the name in your ear". I cried when I heard his voice. I asked him why it had taken him so long for him to find me and when I asked him to stay. He replied; "I will stay with you for as long as you need me" I've gone through a lot of fear with all these new spirits around me and it comforted me to know that Andy was with me now. I trusted him and knew that he would help me.

I continued to meditate every night like clockwork. Grandma and Andy had become very strong with me. Grandma seemed to come less and less now that I had Andy with me. I always felt his presence on my right side. I remember one day I felt frustrated because I talked to him all the time but I had not heard his voice in days. I thought I was forgetting how to hear them. Minutes later I heard someone singing in my head, "How much is that doggie in the window" I thought, what the heck? Then Andy said, "Can you hear me now"? I started laughing and then I realized I can hear them when they want me too. I later learned that it takes a lot of their energy to talk to you. I continued to talk to Andy all day long, and I knew he heard me because he had learned how to poke me. Just like someone was standing beside you poking you in the rib with their finger. He would always poke me when he wanted my attention. The days passed and Andy was always at my side. From the moment I woke up till I went to bed. He was teaching me about spirits and how to communicate with them. The first thing he taught me was that, they will not be tested! They cannot give you proof to help you believe. You must believe first and then they will show you what you believe in. Andy began introducing me to my other spirit guides and helped me to learn from them. The love that I felt when they were with me was incredible. It was a love that I had lacked for a long time. It felt like spirit was breathing life back into me.

I was absorbing everything my Spirit Guides were teaching me, but nothing they taught me compared to my cross over experience. It is a night I will never forget! I have very vivid memories of that night. As if it is etched in my brain forever. I tossed and turned and could feel all the spirits in my room. I knew it was my spirit guides and their presence comforted me as usual.

But this night I had a restless feeling and had a hard time falling asleep. I seemed to be in that in-between state of mind, half awake and half asleep. That is a state they put me in when they want my soul and my conscious to record the experience. I finally fell asleep around 2:00 am, and I seemed to go into a very deep dream state. I crossed over in that dream. I could feel my soul exiting my body and it felt like I was floating thru dimensions of time. When I got to the other side, I remember lying on a table and I could feel spirits all around me. They seemed to be running their hands thru me as if they were cleansing me of all negativity. As I was being cleansed, I started feeling incredible love. With each passing of their hands I felt lighter and lighter.

I could not see them I only felt them and knew they were there. After the cleansing process was complete, I got up from the table and began walking. It was foggy at first as if I were walking thru smoke. I remember beneath me was a fluffiness, as if I were walking on clouds. Off in the distance walking toward me was my grandmother. She appeared the same as I remember her. I felt anxious to get to her, but I could not run. It was if we floated to each other. I embraced her and told her how much I loved her. I could feel her hugging me and it felt so good to see her again. We talked about everything we had missed since her passing. She told me how proud she was of me. The love between us had not changed. It felt as though I was still that little girl years ago.

The fog began to clear and I could see all the beauty around me. I saw a lot of other souls there. I saw my Uncle in the distance and he was with other family members. They were in a boat fishing and joking about whose fish was bigger. I saw some of my other family members and waved to them but did not feel the need to go to them. To the right of me was, what appeared to be a line of souls, waiting for something? In that line, I saw a man that looked familiar. He was my sister-in-laws brother. He had just passed a few days ago. He came to me carrying a teddy bear. I could see the teddy bear clearly. It was tan and the fur was worn out, it had big glass eyes and a black plastic nose. He told me it was the teddy bear that he had when he was little and that his sister needed it now. He told me that she was grieving and needed something to hold. He asked me to give it to her and then handed it to me. There were multiple souls coming to me, telling me who they were and asking me to pass their messages on. Then all of the sudden, I knew what God's plan was for me. The knowing was so strong I could not mistake it. I was to be a messenger for the souls that passed. I knew that I had the ability to walk the line between life and death. Spirits were a part of me and I had been to Heaven before. I was the medium! The person in between, the one that could see and hear both worlds.

I remember asking my grandmother if this was a dream. She smiled and assured me that it was very real and told me to tell my Aunt about this experience. I remember embracing my grandmother again and then I felt something pulling on me. It was gently pulling me backwards. Somehow I knew that it was time to go and I didn't want to leave. I told my grandmother I wanted to stay. She smiled in her gentle way and said my work was only beginning and that I needed to go back. I told her I could not tell my Aunt, that she would think I was crazy. Grandma just repeated… "Tell your Aunt!"

I felt like I was floating back into my body and when I opened my eyes, my fist was still clinched tight to the teddy bear that the spirit had told me to give my sister-in-law. I awoke with a tremendous feeling of love and peace. The love inside me was so strong I trembled and it felt like I would burst if I didn't give it away. I flew out of bed and ran to the phone to call everyone. I called my sister-in-law and told her of my dream and gave her explicit details from her brother. Even though I could not hang onto the teddy bear, I described it to her. Then I called my mother and told her of my visit. She paused as if I were crazy but agreed to pass the message on to her sister (My aunt). After giving everyone their messages I felt on top of the world.

The next day, my sister-in-law called and said she could not find her brother's teddy bear that I had told her about but she did find another stuffed animal to hold and it helped her to feel close to her brother while she grieved. Later that week my mother called me and said she gave the message to my aunt and she said that I was crazy. I felt very disappointed because grandma told me that she would understand.

Two weeks later my Aunt came for a visit and I was very sick, but I knew I had to talk to her. When I got to my mother's house I grabbed my Aunt for a hug and I cried. I could not believe she thought I was crazy. I told her that grandma told me to tell her about it.

She was shocked at what my mother had told me. She did believe me. That's when she told me that my grandmother had the same gift. She started to tell me all the stories of grandma's gift. She said that grandma would dream things and then they would happen just like she dreamed. My grandma was very familiar with the spirits around her. She told me that I had the same gift but my grandma died before she could teach me. I was relieved!

I still to this day, cannot believe how hurtful my mother was. Every message I received that day was validated in some way. I have been receiving messages from spirits ever since. I continued to work with my Spirit Guides on a daily basis. The more I worked with them, the more I wanted. It filled my heart to help people know that their loved ones did not leave them. They are still with us!

I could still feel grandma when she came, but grandma had other people to guide. I felt the spirit of Andy all the time. Andy and I became inseparable and it felt like he was part of me. He knew what I would say before I said it. He was on my mind and in my heart. There were times that I was still afraid; I was still having a lot of panic attacks, sometimes so bad I would go to the hospital. I was getting concerned about the bills I was incurring. Then one day I started to have another attack and all the sudden I could feel Andy's spirit come into me and it calmed me right down. The panic attack stopped!

Andy seemed to be concerned with all my fears and knew it was holding me back spiritually. I still feared death, even though I had already gone through it. So he led me to the book called "Embraced By The Light", written by Betty Eadie. It was her story about her death experience. When I finished reading it, I thought that's it? She made it sound so easy to die. My guides assured me that it wasn't as scary as I was making it out to be. Somehow the book had eased my fears.

A couple nights later, everyone was in bed asleep and I was still up sitting on the sofa. I felt my guides coming in and then Andy made his presence known beside me. Without saying a word, I felt something strange. I felt my energy was being pulled inward. It was a strange feeling like never before. I felt like I was dying and I began to get scared. My mind was speeding up and the thought of my children sleeping in their beds flashed before me. My ex was sleeping as well and the feeling of my soul being drawn in was getting stronger. I kept thinking, I am dying and nobody knows. Who will find my body? What will my children do without me? And all of the sudden my spirit ejected from my body. I was floating about six foot in front of my body. I knew my body was sitting on the couch behind me but I could not turn around to see. I could feel all my guides around me with much more awareness. I was focused on the awareness that even though I died. I still exist. All my memories and thoughts are still there. I was very aware of my being. Then I was sucked very quickly backwards and slammed back into my body. I gasped for breath and shouted out, "Don't ever do that again!" I was angry with my guides for scaring me like that. I really thought I was dying.

The next day when I had calmed down, I asked the guides why they hadn't told me that it was only practice. They responded that had I known ahead of time, I would not have experienced it in full. I understand now but I was still upset when it happened. It made me realize that the death process isn't that bad. We just fear the unknown.

Andy told me that my soul leaves my body every night while I am sleeping. He said he takes me places and shows me things and sometimes he takes me dancing in the realm.

One night as I started to fall asleep, he came to me and said he would help me out of my body and was taking me dancing. I said no, not until I was asleep. I could feel him gently pulling on my spirit, as if to coax me. I could feel my energy moving and I shouted no again. I didn't want to feel it. I told him to let me go to sleep first. He just laughed and let me go to sleep. He was trying to help me let my fear go.

In the weeks ahead, my children thought that my ability was cool. They could both feel Andy's spirit and wanted to learn. I thought about all the fear I went through and said no. They kept pressing and said that they did not fear it. The next thing I know Andy started working with them and had opened their ability. My son seemed to progress over night, and my daughters process was a little more gradual. Seeing that my kids were not afraid somehow eased my fear as well. I guess Andy knew what he was doing.

As the months passed, I continued to have problems with my ex husband. He did not like what I was doing and kept telling me I was crazy. Ever since my brain surgery, he had accused me of being possessed and he forbid me to talk to dead people, (as he called them). I had enough and went outside on the patio. I loved helping people and this was my path now. I was angry that he was trying to take that away from me. I raised my hands to God and prayed for him to make me stronger with him.

Then the voice came again, "I cannot make your light stronger when you live in such darkness" The voice was right, my ex husband was so negative and he was holding me back spiritually. He said I was not the same person he married. I knew that if I wanted to grow closer to God and do his work I had to leave. The love between us had died long ago. Spirit promised that I would never be alone and they promised to work with me and make me stronger if I took that step forward with them.

Spirit was right. My children had grown now and I was hanging onto a broken relationship with no love. So I made arrangements to move on with my life. It was a decision I never regretted.

$\mathcal{S}pirits\ \mathcal{P}romise$

S PIRIT KEPT THEIR promise and was always by my side. My spirit guides gave me a couple months to grieve for my marriage and then began working with me. Every day they came to me and practiced. They would let me feel them and then they would move around the room, asking me to point them out. This exercise made my sense of feel stronger. They would talk to me and sing songs in my head to help me to hear them better. They have shown me over and over again that we do hear them; we just need to know what to listen for. We do not hear them with our ears, rather a thought that they put in our head (telepathically). It took some training to listen with my mind and to know the difference between my thoughts and theirs. After months of exercising my senses, they rewarded me by showing themselves to me. In a flash, the room lit up and I could see them as if they were standing right there in full detail. It only lasted briefly, but it was etched in my mind. Then they strengthened my mind's eye, showing me signs and symbols that I would need to do readings.

They never let me feel alone and helped me to grow stronger spiritually. My guides led me to a small spiritual church a few months before I left my ex, and I had made some friends that were spiritual like me. I spent a lot of time with them and learned of there experiences with their spirit guides. Once again I thirst for more. I wanted to learn everything. I remember one of the girls from the church coming for a visit and she was talking about the Mother God. I was caught off guard by this statement. I was brought up in a Christian faith and never taught about a Mother God. I remembered reading a book by Sylvia Brown, and she had mentioned Mother God as well. My guides always taught me to discern the information I was hearing. So I turned to God and prayed for the answers. I prayed for two days and on the third day I was sitting in my chair and I felt a holy presence in my room. I felt Andy and my guides bowing their heads to the presence of this spirit and when I tried to look up to see who it was, Andy gently pushed my head down. All of the sudden I could see it; the walls seemed to open up in my apartment and I saw this beautiful female presence coming toward me. She was escorted by many angels and high spirits. I remember asking who she was and the most loving voice said: "I am Mother". I bowed my head lower and was in awe. I had often questioned the bible when it says we are created in the image of the father. I thought, but I am a girl. Mother answered "You my child were created in my image, as all females are". I remember feeling bad because I did not know. I asked for her forgiveness and she said "Go forth my child and teach the people that I exist." I felt her energy pulling back and the walls seemed to close behind her. That was a very profound experience for me and I have included Mother God in my prayers ever since. Adding her to my prayers has proven to be even more powerful and effective.

Andy and my spirit guides continued to teach me every day. Day after day they showed me what they were capable of. Just when I thought I had seen everything, they would show me something new. I was on my way to work one day and running late. My day was already starting out bad and as I drove down the road I hear "Wow, Look at the butt crack". I looked up and there was a guy riding a bike in front of me and his butt crack was showing. I laughed so hard I cried. I had not noticed before he said that. That's just one of the ways they can turn your day around.

I was in the back shop at work one day, taking a break and my attention was drawn to a coiled up hose hanging on the wall. All of the sudden Andy made the hose bounce. I had been asking him if he could move things and he said yes, but would never do it. Again, they will not be tested! When you least expect it, they will show you. Another time at work, I was really busy doing the books and the fax machine kept ringing and spitting out junk mail. It was a distraction to me so I reached over and shut it off. The next day I was sitting at my desk working and I received a text mail on my phone. I don't text and thought it was strange. I looked at my phone to see who sent it and it came from my cell phone. That was strange, I didn't text myself? I clicked on the message and it said; "don't forget to turn your fax machine on". I had completely forgot that I had shut it off the day before and when I turned it on, there were three orders waiting to come thru. I cried when I realized they could send you messages. Just another way they can communicate.

Andy continued to amaze me. I remembered the three times he saved my life. I had slipped on some ice going out to my car and my feet went out from under me. I was going down fast. All of the sudden, I felt his spirit move under me. He caught me, lifted me back to my feet and held me until I got my balance. I said thank you in amazement, and Andy said "My pleasure". Another time I stopped at a garage sale, I pulled over on the opposite side of the road to park. I got out of the car and looked both ways to cross. Just as I stepped into the road, I felt him grab the back of my shirt and yank me backwards. Just as I looked up, a truck was speeding past. I never saw it coming.

The one I will never forget was when I was driving home from work when a car had sped out of a side street and had come across three lanes of traffic into my lane and was coming head on with me. It happened so fast I did not have time to react. Andy grabbed the wheel and without hitting the car beside me and avoiding going up over the curb, he had brought me to safety. I still don't know how he did that, but I continue to thank him for it.

I was growing even closer to Andy now. He was with me through good times and bad. He taught me to trust him, he had given me the strength to leave a bad marriage, and he had been my teacher and confidant through everything.

One day, as I was driving to work, I was listening to a love song on the radio and thinking about him. His loving voice came into my head and he whispered, "Get ready to fall in love". I thought for a minute and said; "I already am"! I had already fallen deeply in love with him. I know he is a spirit, but I could feel him as if he was physical, I could hear him talking to me and I trusted him with all my heart.

Over the next few months I became so close to him that I felt him with all of my soul. I knew what he was thinking. I could feel his love for me and he held me in his embrace as I fell asleep and he was there with me when I awoke. I never thought I could love anyone so much. This was the love that I had waited so long for. He would come to me all the time and give me love. Love on the other side is much different. When his spirit gives me love, I would feel this beautiful wave of warm calming love start from my head and flow to my toes. Once again, there are no words for how it made me feel. It truly was a Heavenly experience.

One night while I was lying in my bed, I became focused on Andy's spirit embracing me. I felt a seriousness coming from his energy. Just then, he opened my hand and I could feel a slight heaviness as he laid something in my palm. Before I could ask what it was, he showed me his heart. He whispered that he had always loved me and now his love had grown even deeper. He promised to love me for eternity. The giving of his heart touched me to the core of my soul and I knew that I felt the same way. We were meant to be one. I vowed my love to his spirit that night and it is a night I will never forget.

The next day it was back to work as usual. Andy continued to teach me how to astral project and how to do remote viewing. I would think of where I wanted to go and will myself to go there. One day I willed myself to my mom's house and Andy told me to pay close attention to details. I could feel myself there in the room with her. I saw that she was wearing her pink flowered pajamas and was sitting in her favorite chair watching TV. I looked to see what she was watching and what she was doing. Then I willed myself back home. When I opened my eyes and was back in my chair, I shrugged it off and thought; well those were just my memories of what mom usually does. So Andy convinced me to call my mom. I asked her why she was still in her pajamas this time of day. I also told her I didn't like the pots and pans that they were selling on the QVC. (That's the channel that she was watching.) She got a little freaked out and wondered how I knew all of that. She accused me of hiding somewhere in her house and playing a practical joke. I had fun with that one.

My M.S. Would get bad sometimes and Andy always knew when I was having a bad spell. He would comfort me with his love and call in some healing spirits to help. No matter where I was, Andy would come to me and flip my hands over to expose my palms. This warm energy would start coming into the palms of my hands and I could feel the energy going through my whole body. I would just close my eyes and absorbed every bit of it until it was gone. I was very sensitive to drugs and had developed a lot of side effects from them so I chose not to be medicated. I prayed to God for healing of this disease and to help me find a treatment that was comfortable. His answer to me was palms up! The palms of your hands are your receivers. The healing energy starts out warm and gets hotter. You just have to have faith and receive Gods energy. That has always brought me a lot of comfort in sick times.

The Readings

I CONTINUED TO work with Andy and my guides every day and the day came that I felt ready to deliver messages. I was at work and one of my favorite salesmen came in. He was a happy man and always telling jokes. Not this day, he seemed very down and when I asked what was wrong, he told me that his son had committed suicide and that his wife blamed herself and was giving up on life. I told him about my gift and as he was listening to me he got Goosebumps. Goosebumps are spirits way of getting you to pay attention. I told him to bring his wife to me and I would see if his son would come through in a reading. Later that weekend they came to my home and I began the reading.

I could feel Andy and my guides come into the room and as I began to tune in, I could feel her son's presence. He came through so strong that day. He told me to tell his mom that it was not a suicide. He explained that he had been at a party and had a bit to much too drink. His friends had convinced him to try drugs and without knowing what he was doing, he had accidentally overdosed. He told her she was a good mother and that he would be watching over her now. He answered all her questions and then another spirit came in. It was her twin brother that had passed in the war. I knew it was her twin because he looked just like her. He showed me a plane going down and crashing. She validated that he died in a plane crash. He continued to give her validations that only she would know, and then told her he would give her a sign when he was with her. When the reading was over she was happy and excited. My job was done and I realized how much people needed to hear from their loved ones and it brought me joy to help her.

Two weeks later the salesman came back and thanked me for helping. He told me that I had saved his wife. Now that she had gotten closure, she could move on with her life and looked forward to loved ones giving her signs.

That was my first reading and it gave me a good feeling to know that I helped. I continued to give readings in the years to come. Each reading was unique in its own way. Spirits always knew what they needed to heal and were eager to guide them. I don't remember most of my readings. When I am channeling spirits energy the messages are for them and unless it touches me in some way, I usually don't remember them.

I had done many readings over a two year period but it became harder to do them at my apartment. I had assigned parking with few guest spots and people would get turned around in the complex. I had to find a place more convenient to do my readings so I checked into the library and found that I could rent a room there to do my readings. That worked for awhile but there were too many distractions from people walking past the windows and looking in. I knew I had to do something different. So a few months later I bought a home located in the middle of the city. It was right off the exit to the highway and was really easy to find. When I was unpacked and settled, my spirit guides came to me and asked me to go public. The idea of going public terrified me. I was very shy, I didn't handle criticism well and I lived alone. After some gentle nudging and constant support from my guides, I finally put myself out there for the public. Things were slow at first, but once I got started the word of mouth just flowed. Like dropping a pebble in the water and watching the ripple effect. After a few months I had people calling me from all over the state. I was trying to balance my two jobs and find time for my readings but I was happy and content.

With God's guidance, Andy at my side and my guides helping me to understand the messages I was growing stronger. The signs and symbols kept coming and my clients were getting a kick out of Andy poking me so much. Andy knew I was nervous before every reading so he would ease my fear by poking me in the ribs during the readings. I had to explain to my clients why I was jerking and grunting so much. The readings were one thing, but when I am standing in line at a grocery store and he starts poking me, everyone is looking at me like, what's wrong with her? My face would turn red and I would just put my head down, trying not to be noticed while I was scolding Andy in my head for embarrassing me. He had such a cute laugh that I could not stay mad at him long.

One day I had a very sweet woman come for a reading and it was one that would change my perspective. During the reading, a female came through and I felt the kind of love that only soul mates have. It is a powerful love that cannot be denied. Her lover had taken her own life because she was a professional and was afraid of someone finding out about her love life. She tried to resist her feelings, but they were too strong so she ended up taking her own life. I remember that during the reading, the client had burst into tears and had reached out to touch my face. While I was channeling she could see her lovers face within mine and she needed to touch her one last time. The spirit gave her many validations during the reading, but the one that really made her a believer was when the spirit called her by the nick name she had given her. That was a very emotional reading for me. I not only felt their love for each other, but their emotions as well.

I had asked God many times about same sex relationships and he answered me in this reading. I felt the power of their love and I knew that it was too strong to resist it. I questioned why God would put soul mates in the same sex body if it were wrong? My answer was that God is love and our purpose on this earth is to love and be loved. It is not up to us to judge!

I found that a lot of my clients were going through abuse and infidelity just as I had. I look back on my life and all that I had gone through, often questioning why that happened to me. I think the answer was that I needed to experience it and learn from it so that I could guide my clients through it.

I read for a lady one day and her mother had come through in spirit. She was showing me that her daughter was being abused. I could see what she had been through and what was going to happen. She validated everything in the past. Then her mother showed me her lying in a hospital bed and I felt it was going to happen soon. I told her what her mom had shown me and she just shrugged it off. She said that she loved him and could not leave him. Two days later, she called me from the hospital and he had beaten her just like her mom had shown me in a vision. I always feel like I have somehow failed getting the message across when I cannot prevent bad things from happening. My guides explained to me that it is my job to give the messages and leave it with them. As much as I wish I could, I cannot change their will.

Most of my readings were positive and healing. I had always told my guides that I did not want to be one of those psychics that will tell you bad things, but

I remember the day I got something bad. I was reading for a client and everything was going good until she asked the question about her health. As I looked at her, my guides showed me a black mass in her left breast. I swallowed hard and refused to give it. My guides kept repeating it over and over and told me to tell her. This is the first time that ever happened. So I looked at her and asked if she wanted to know everything. She said yes, so I cautiously told her what I saw. I told her I had never seen that before and to please get it checked out by her doctor. It felt horrible to deliver that message and I was angry with my guides for making me give it. A year later she came to me again and I remembered her face. I hugged her and apologized for giving her a bad message. She cried and said Thank you! She told me it was because I had given her the message that she went to the doctor and they were able to catch it in time. She went through surgery and chemo and now she was healthy. Once again, I apologized for being angry with my guides for making me give that message. I realized that they will only show me something bad if it can be changed.

I've seen cancer a few more times in my readings and every time spirit showed it to me it saved the clients life. The one time I could not save a life, it hit close to home. My dad had been having problems urinating and spirit showed me the cancer in him. Without telling him what I saw, I convinced him to have his prostate checked out.

My dad hated doctors and had only been to them a few times in his life. I went to the doctor with him that day to express my concerns. They agreed to do a biopsy and we waited weeks for the results.

The biopsy results came back negative for cancer. My guides kept telling me that they missed it. I told dad we needed to do it again, but he had gone through so much the first time that he did not want to repeat it. As much as it was killing me inside, I had to respect his wishes. Eight months later he got worse and went to the doctor again.

They found the cancer and this time it had spread into his bladder and kidneys. Dad was in a frail state now and they could not do surgery. I went to the hospital to visit him and when I walked into the room, I saw my grandmother and grandfathers spirit with him. I swallowed hard and tried not to cry, I knew that I had to be strong for dad. I walked over to his bed and kissed him. He looked up at me and said "they were telling him it was time to go somewhere, but didn't know how to get there". I hugged my dad and cried. I knew it was close if he was seeing and hearing them because he did not have my ability.

I told him to not be afraid, that when the time came, they would guide his way. A few days later I was sitting at my dining room table when I had a strong feeling of my dad and I felt him let go of life. I cried and then I felt my spirit rise up. I was guiding him to the other side. I could see it in my mind. I told him I loved him and to remember that I would always feel him and hear him. Fifteen minutes later I got the call from the hospital telling me that he had passed at the exact time I felt him. Twelve minutes later his spirit came back to me and asked "How long did it take"? I looked at the clock and said 12 minutes. Dad said "I told you I would beat her" I laughed and cried at the same time because I remembered a year earlier when his sister had passed, he called to give me the sad news and asked me to call him when she got to the other side. 18 minutes later her spirit came to me and said to tell dad that she had made it to Heaven and that she was alright. I called my dad and gave him the message. He told me that when his time came he would beat her. It was a cute little competition they had going. My dad doesn't come to me very often, because when I feel his loving spirit I always get emotional.

Andy and my guides continued to comfort me through the grief of losing my father, and he even brought him to me a few times. I took some time off from work and readings and when I was ready, they continued to work with me. Andy and I's love for each other had grown beyond words. I vowed my heart to him and was content with loving his spirit, but sometimes when I would walk in the park and see couples holding hands and kissing, it made me miss the physical part of him. Even though

I was so in love and happy, Andy knew that I lacked the physical needs.

I was sitting at home one night when Andy came to me and told me to go out for a drink. He knew I did not get out much and I certainly did not drink. But he was insistent, so I called a friend and asked her if she wanted to go out. While I was getting dressed, Andy told me to wear something nice. When I asked why he said that I would see him there. I was confused and excited; I didn't know what he was talking about.

I picked my friend up and we drove to the local pub that Andy had told me about. When I walked in, my spirit guides turned my attention to a man sitting in the corner. My heart sank and I could not take my eyes off him. The man looked so much like Andy. My girlfriend and I sat down a few tables away and ordered a drink. I found myself staring at the man in the corner. Then our eyes met and locked. I smiled and he smiled back. The next thing I know he is walking over to our table. He struck up a conversation and I apologized for staring so much. I told him that he looked a lot like someone I loved that had passed away. He took that as a compliment and continued talking about how lucky that man was to have me. Minutes went by and all of the sudden I could see Andy's spirit looking through his eyes. I could feel Andy's loving energy as he reached for my hand, and at that moment time seemed to stop and nothing else existed. We just sat there locked on each other's eyes. He told me how beautiful I was and that he wishes he could be with me. Then one of his friends came in and yelled his name and the trance was broken. He went back to his table to join his friend. We exchanged a few more glances that night and I've never seen that man again.

When I got back home, I asked Andy how that happened and Andy explained to me that they can channel through someone, just as I do in my readings. It's when a spirit merges with a physical body and uses them to speak or to touch someone. Even though I do it all the time in my readings, I have never had it done to me before. Once again I was amazed by what they can do. It reminded me of the time my client saw her loved one in my face and needed to touch my cheek. It helped me to understand how channeling works.

Andy has only shown himself physically three times. The first time I saw him I was at the mall. I saw him walking toward me and when he smiled at me my heart sank. I kept trying to convince myself that it couldn't be him. I asked my guides if it was him and they didn't say a word. The next thing I know he had already passed me and when I turned around to look, he was gone. The other time I was driving to work and I happened to look in my rear view mirror and saw him sitting in the middle of the back seat smiling at me. I stared at him in the mirror with amazement and then I realized I was driving and needed to watch the road. When I looked back he was gone. The last time I saw him I had sprained my ankle and had just woke up. I bent down to put my splint on and when I looked up he was standing in the doorway of my bedroom. It was so real I could almost touch him. But when I got up he was gone. Each time he shows himself it makes me yearn for more. I have learned that it takes a lot of their energy to show themselves in a physical state, so it doesn't happen very often.

The Walk In

THE EXPERIENCE OF Andy channeling through someone and showing himself to me, stayed with me and made me miss the physical touch even more. Then one day Andy came to me and said he needed to be with me. I laughed and said you already are. He said it wasn't the same, he needed to be able to touch me and hold me physically. I thought how was that possible? He was in spirit. He talked to me through the night explaining that there was a way for him to be physical and that it was dangerous but he was willing to give up Heaven to be with me. The next day he led me to a book called "Strangers among us", written by Ruth Montgomery. I read every word of that book and learned that they can come back here to earth without going through the womb. The book explained that they have to find a person that no longer wants to be here on this earth. The heavenly soul talks to the physical soul and gets permission. It has to be agreed upon by both souls. Then a transition takes place.

The spirit comes into the physical body during sleep, and the physical soul goes to a holding place on the other side. During the days of transition, the spirit will become accustomed to the body and all the memories of that person's life. While the physical soul that is in holding gets used to the light and love of heaven and they can hear their loved ones talking to them. When they are both ready and sure that it is what they want, God will cut the cord to the body releasing the physical soul to heaven and the new spirit soul then becomes attached to the body. This process is called a "walk in" and it saves the time of being born again. The whole process can take up to four months to complete.

I was afraid for Andy to do this because there were dangers involved. He assured me that he had done it before in another life and he was confident he could do it again with God's help. He said that he had already found someone willing to do this. He spent that night holding me and letting me feel his love and the next day when I woke up, he was gone. My grandmother was now at my side guiding me while Andy was in transition.

I missed him terribly and was grieving for him. My grandmother tried to console me over the next couple weeks. I kept thinking of him and trying to get used to what it would be like to hold him for the first time. A month had passed and I asked grandma how he was doing. She started to tell me things about him. Where he lived, what he done for a living and she told me that the soul he was replacing has lost his wife a year before and the man had lost his will to live. I asked how I would meet him and she told me that he would find me. Andy had worked hard and was half way through the transition when grandma came to me and said he would be calling me for a reading that night. My heart sank and I thought what do I say to him? He will have no memory of who he is or what happened to him. Later that night my phone rang and when I answered the phone he hung up. I was devastated and thought I had lost my opportunity. Grandma came to me the next day and told me it would not work. She said that everything had to be right. The timing had to be perfect, and they found out that the man Andy was transitioning with would have rejected me because of my gift. She told me that Andy would pull out.

The next day I felt Andy's spirit with me. He was very weak and I could hardly feel him, but he was back. I told him it was okay. I felt like I was dying inside without him and I would just love him in spirit just as I had been. He told me he would try again when he got his strength back and I told him NO! I did not want to go through that again. The nights of crying and missing him had emotionally drained me, not to mention how weak he was from the experience.

It amazes me to know what spirits have the ability to do. So I began asking more questions and my guides were more than willing to answer. I was so grateful that

Andy had loved me so much that he was willing to give up Heaven to come here on earth, and I told them that I would have made the same sacrifice to be with him. My guides told me that we had both done it several times in past lives.

Again, the more they taught me, the more I wanted to know. I was starting to get clients that were asking me about merging. Their husbands had passed and they had finally decided to move on with their life. Every once in a while they said they could feel the touch of there deceased husband through the new man they were with. My experience with Andy gave me a certainty that it was truly happening. Our loved ones simply merge with a physical body that is willing, so they can touch us again. Just like the scene in the movie "Ghost", where Patrick Swayze merges with Whoopi to be able to touch his girl one more time. It really happens! Again to make it clear, the souls have to be given permission, a spirit cannot just merge or transition into someone that is not willing.

Our loved ones never leave us. They are always around us and giving us signs that they are there. The souls in heaven do not miss us because they are with us. We are their Heaven and they are drawn to the love we have for them. There is no time on the other side, so they know they will see us again in a blink of an eye. We, the physical souls. Are the ones that are stuck in this place of time and gravity. But spirit has shown me that even though we are physical we can still do what spirit does.

Just not to the same degree. Spirits travel at the speed of thought. They think about us and they are there beside us. If they miss having coffee, they think about it and can taste it, as if they were having a cup. Spirit does not thirst or hunger, but if they desire something, they can create it with their thoughts. God makes everything available to them. Just like when I crossed over and saw my uncle fishing. He loved to fish and was anxious to show me that he still can. All he has to do is will it for himself.

Spirit has taught me that we create everything with our minds, just as God created the world. We are made in the image of our father, the creator, and that means that we are all little creators.

Spirits continued to show me that our mind is powerful. We just need to will it for ourselves. Months later, a book called "The Secret" hit the book shelves. I remember reading it and getting emotional. The book was everything that my guides had taught me for years. Visualize it and make it happen. It can be done! If we all just loved one another and sent that positive energy out there, what we visualize could change the world.

I became very excited with all that spirit was teaching me and was being led to teach others. So I started teaching classes. Spirit was eager to guide every session. Over the weeks I guided their meditations and watched as people opened up to God and connected with their guides. By the end of the fourth class they were giving me messages. It warmed my heart to see them connect with their loved ones and being guided through their daily lives.

Every piece of information Spirit gave me would come up in my readings or help me with classes. More and more I would see the evidence of miracles around me. I was grateful for all spirit had given me and happy to teach it to others. I could see the positive changes in people.

Then one day I got a call from a desperate mother. Her son had tried to commit suicide three times and swore he was going to do it again. He told her he didn't want to be here anymore. The mother was frantic and asked if I could help her son. A rush of spirit energy came over me and I told her to bring him to me. Two days later he was at my door. He came in and sat down, and began telling me that he had read the book "Strangers Among Us", and that he had asked God to take him out of this world. He kept telling me that God would not hear his prayers. When he said that I felt the Holy Spirit merge with me and I slid to the front of my chair. I began to shake from the energy that was coming through me and I began to speak to him in a voice that was not mine. Spirit told him that they had not forsaken him and that his prayers were heard.

The boy said that he was gay and that he was tired of being picked on and not being excepted by others. He had been asking God for a walk in so he could exit and when it didn't happen he decided to take himself out. At that moment his face changed and I saw another soul imposed upon him. I knew that he had already been walked into. I explained to the boy that his soul was already on the other side. I explained how it works and told him that he has no memory of it because the new souls mind is washed when they become physical. I told him that was one of the dangers of a walk in. They take over the memory of the previous soul and think they are them, they have no idea that it has already happened. Then spirit came into me and my voice changed again and told him that his mission was to go forth and mentor other boys. All the sudden his mood changed, and it was as if he finally understood his mission. He promised to stop trying to kill himself and do the task at hand. His mother called me several weeks later and thanked me for the help. She said her son's life had changed and he was a completely different person and was now involved with a program to help guide others.

I have seen it several times since then. When I ask how often this happens, God shows me parachutes coming down to earth. Hundreds of souls coming down and transitioning into physical bodies. When this happens there is a total personality change, and they are driven forward by their spirit guides to make a difference in this world. Then it dawned on me, I had changed the day of my brain surgery and when I came home everything was strange to me. I felt very different and was doing things that I normally would not do. I stood up to my ex when I normally would have cowered to him, and I finally had the strength to leave him for good. When I had left so many times before only to come back home again. I remembered him telling me that I had changed and that I wasn't the same person anymore.

It all made sense now. My world was crashing then, my marriage was falling apart again and I remember praying to God to take me home. I was unloved and had lost my will to live. I seen the loving face of Jesus that day just before they had put me under. I died on the table and woke up feeling strange. Spirit had led me to the medium show that day to form my path and they were strong with me through all of it. I went through the fear and confusion and I found strength in my faith to overcome it. I had all the signs of a walk in then, so I asked my guides. Did I have a walk in that day? There was a pause and then came the answer. Yes! I made a transition that day.

Andy came to me one night and said he had to leave. He said he had taught me as much as he could and he needed to turn me over to a new teacher. I was pleading with him not to go, but he said his soul needed to go forward to progress. I told him that he was the only one that I trusted and asked who would be taking his place. He raised my head and Jesus was standing in front of me. He told me I needed to start working with Jesus. I was afraid that I wasn't worthy of Jesus. Jesus came to me for two days and I cried, feeling unworthy both times. On the third day Jesus came to me again and this time, he lifted my head and said: "Bow not unto me for I cannot teach you with your head down. Lift your head and walk beside me so that I may teach you".

Two days later Jesus came to Andy and I and we knelt before him. Jesus placed his hands upon our heads and joined us. We were now one with each other. I had already vowed my love to Andy a long time ago and had wanted it to be so. Later that night after meditation I was led to go and get my picture of Jesus. He had me place it on my lap and look into his beautiful eyes. I seemed to stare at his loving face for hours. Mesmerized by the love and comfort that I felt in his eyes. That night I remember Andy holding me all night long and in the morning when I awoke, Andy was gone.

Jesus was standing beside my bed and told me that I was dying. I wasn't afraid when he told me that, but I asked how much time I had left because I needed to prepare my children. He never answered me. Later that day, I was told that the Andy I knew existed no more. Jesus told me that Andy would always be in my heart. I cried and kept asking where Andy was. Did he leave me or was he reborn?

Three days later, I was told by my guides that Andy was doing another walk in. I remember feeling my soul dying the last time he was separated from me and did not know if I had the strength to get through it again, but I felt comforted in knowing Jesus was with me this time. Andy knew my soul would parish without him and if I died before he could find me, his transition would all be for nothing. I knew that spirit would not let that happen, so I stayed in my faith.

A few weeks later, a female spirit came to me. She told me that she was the wife of the physical man that Andy was transitioning with. She merged with me to get to know my heart and she agreed to let Andy use her husband's body to love me. She only had one request. She asked if she could use me to keep her memory alive with her son and grand children. I told her I would be honored and she was gone.

The months passed and I was grieving for Andy horribly. I could feel my soul dying inside. I was hurting so bad, I remember praying to God to make the pain go away. I desperately needed to find Andy or I would not survive. Soul mates will parish without each other. Once again, the loving voices told me to hang on and they started giving me updates of Andy's transition every day to keep me hopeful. I drew my close friends even closer, and relied on them a lot. They knew that Andy was transitioning and checked on me every day to make sure I was alright. They would pray with me and try to get me out of the house. I was slipping deeper and deeper into depression and was losing my will to live. If I did not find Andy soon it would be too late.

Then my guides came to me and said Andy was complete. He was fully in body now and they were working on the time for us to meet. They told me he lived close by, and what kind of car that he drove, and they showed me what kind of house he had. They said his wife had passed away a year ago and that he had lost his will to live. They told me everything about him. I asked them how much longer and they replied, he was still grieving and needed more time.

During my meditations spirit would open that connection between us and I could feel him. I knew what he was doing and how he was feeling. That gave me hope. Spirit assured me that once I met him it would move swiftly. We would fall in love and be married in a short time. I asked how will I know it's my love when I meet him. My guides replied you will see his soul when you look into his eyes.

A couple weeks later I was going to my friend's wedding. Part of me did not want to go to a happy occasion when I was so sad, but spirit kept guiding me to go. She too had to wait for her soul mate to transition and she had already found him and they were getting married. I knew I had to go and help them celebrate their love. While I was getting dressed to go, my guides came to me and told me to wear something nice. I did not think anything of it, of course I would dress nice, it was a wedding. As I was driving to the wedding a strange feeling came over me and I began shaking. I had a feeling that I might meet my love there, but my guides would not give me validation. I got to the wedding and checked on my friend to see if she needed anything. Then I went in to sit down. As the people gathered in the room I felt the energy of someone walking down the aisle behind me. It was a man rolling out the silk mat. I could feel his embarrassment as he was trying to roll out the mat because it kept getting hung up on the rope. I looked at the man and said; "it don't look like your having much fun," and he said they had asked him to roll the mat at the last minute and he didn't know what he was doing.

I smiled at him hoping it would make his day better and then he was gone. I looked for him during the wedding but did not see him again. The night went on and I had twisted my ankle walking through the parking lot and it was hurting, so I decided to leave early.

I got home and was feeling disappointed that I did not meet my love. A week later, my friend got home from her honeymoon and called to tell me that they were going to introduce me to someone that night but didn't get the chance because I left early. I told her I did not want to be set up because I was waiting for my love. She then told me that her husband had a friend that needed a reading and wanted me to come to dinner on the weekend. It was my birthday that Saturday and she said she would bake a cake for dessert. I agreed to go and give their friend a reading.

Saturday came and when I got to my friends house he was not there yet. We sat down to talk and looked at the wedding pictures. Moments later there was a knock at the door and he had arrived. When I looked up, I recognized him as the man that was struggling to roll out the mat. We laughed about that day and then sat down to dinner. After dinner, he was waiting for his reading and wanted it to be private, so we went to the kitchen table while everyone else waited in the living room.

The reading started and his wife's spirit came through first. Giving him messages of love and validation, then his father, his step dad, all of his grandparents and even a friend had come thru to say hello and give him messages. He just sat there in disbelief and later told me that he was a skeptic and did not believe in mediums, but he had an open mind. He was blown away at the validations that came thru that day. I had turned a skeptic into a believer that day. He thanked me and said "wow", I want to do this again, so I handed him a business card. The next day, he called me and asked me out for dinner. I declined his invitation because I did not want a date I just wanted to help him through his grief. Spirit told me that he would call again and said it would not hurt to be friends. The next time he called I agreed to go to dinner as a friend. We went to dinner and had a wonderful time. I was so nervous that I talked constantly. I had been single for nine years now and had never been on a date. My guides kept reminding me to let him talk. I had looked into his eyes a few times that night and all I saw was darkness. It was the pain from everything he went through. When he brought me home he gave me a hug and thanked me for the evening.

The next day he called and asked me out for a second date and then a third. We were getting along great and having a good time. He always made me laugh and I felt comfortable with him. On the fourth date, I looked into his eyes and this time I could see the color of his eyes and I started to feel his soul. There was a slight connection there but I still was not sure. So I started asking him questions about the signs that spirit had told me. He answered all the questions correctly. When I got home that night, my guides came to me and said: "He is the one you're looking for". I asked again to make sure I heard was correctly. I got excited and I could not believe that my love had found me. It had been 4 months since Andy left me.

We talked on the phone everyday getting to know each other and counting down to our next date. One month had passed and we were talking on the phone one night and he said he had no intention of falling in love again and I replied the same. He told me that he had been fighting his feelings back, but no matter how hard he resisted, he had fallen madly in love with me. I felt the exact same way. I knew that if God was bringing us together we could not resist. We went out again that weekend and you could not separate us after that. I had waited so long for him and I could not bear another day without him.

Two weeks later, on Thanksgiving day with my children present, he asked me to marry him and two short months later we were married in front of God and our children. The love between us was incredible. When Andy said he needed to touch me, he was not kidding. He is always touching me. He is either holding my hand or touching my leg. He is my one and only! "There was no doubt in my mind that he is the one. Everything about him is Andy. From his personality to his likes and his passions". I had found my love and it happened just like my spirit guides told me it would. What a miracle!

His family members kept saying how much he had changed. They said that he was not the same man anymore. It's like he is a different person and they had never seen him so happy. They said he was doing things that he never would have done in the past and they told me that I had changed his life! I can't take credit for that. It was not me that changed him. Or was it? Only God knows!

The Shocking Reveal

MY HUSBAND AND I have been happily married for three years now and life couldn't be better. We had a few struggles in the beginning with the merging of our families, but with God's help and time, we have all come together and have formed a close bond. Life has presented us some changes; I am retired now due to my M.S. And a year later my husband retired so he could spend more time with me.

After we got married, I continued to feel Andy's energy and love within my husband. I could not believe how he and Andy were so much alike and my husband had often told me how similar I am to his first wife. He told me that she too had some level of psychic. She often knew what was going to happen and had a good judge of people. She suffered greatly over the years with her weight, MRSA and skin cancer. We both had bad childhoods growing up and she struggled with depression as well. In the end she was very sick and overwhelmed with depression and just gave up on life.

After I retired from my job, I continued to serve God through my readings and teaching classes. My Spirit Guides gave me the inspiration to write a book about my life. So I sat at my computer day and night for weeks on end, typing as the words and memories flowed into my head. When the book was on its final chapter and nearing the end. I felt a release of all the pain that I had experienced during my childhood. I sent it off to the publisher and within a week I got word back that it had been rejected due to content. Even though it didn't get published, I was glad that I had written it because it helped me to let a lot of my past go and I can start healing now.

A few days after the book was rejected I woke up in the morning feeling really weak. Something just didn't feel right. I began missing Andy so bad that I began to cry. It was as if I was thrown back in time three years ago, to the day he left me. I kept thinking to myself, why was I missing Andy? My husband is here and everything is fine, but for some reason I couldn't stop crying. My mind felt like it was in a fog and all I could think about was Andy. Within a few minutes I could feel my spirit guides coming in. My soul started to speak to me. I kept saying "why did I have to come back?" Where was Andy? I felt separated from him and it felt like I was dying again. I was so confused… At that moment my guides spoke and told me that it was time for me to come back, but would say no more. I thought back from where? Where had I been? I didn't understand! I could not talk to my husband about this because he wouldn't understand and I didn't want to upset him. So I went to my daughter's house. She and my son both have the gift like me and communicate with their Guides, so I hoped that she could get some answers from her guides.

When I got there, I hugged her and started to cry so hard I could not speak. She hugged me and said "Oh my God mom, your Back!" I looked at her in shock and asked her what she was talking about. She sat me down and after calming me, she began to explain. She said that four years ago when I was grieving for the loss of Andy, she could feel me slipping away. She knew I hurt so bad that I didn't want to be here without him.

Then one night while she was sleeping, she felt my soul leave and go to Heaven. Just like I felt my dad when he passed. She was devastated. The next morning, after her dream, she called me and when she heard my voice she said I was different and she still felt that I had passed into Heaven that night. Even though she was seeing and talking to me, she knew it wasn't me. She said that somehow the connection between us was gone and we have always been close.

She was so excited to have me back. I asked her, "why did I come back"? She said it was because she and the grand children needed me. I was angry at first. If I was in Heaven with Andy then why did I have to come back, and where was Andy? We talked for a long while and soon everything made sense. I could start to feel Andy's spirit with me but he was weak and I was feeling the same way. He had helped to guide my spirit back into body and we were both weak from the transition. My need for answers faded away once I knew that Andy was still with me. I knew that Spirit would answer my questions when they were ready.

In the days ahead my guides began to reveal everything to me. They took me back to the time when I was grieving. When my husband's first wife came to me in spirit and said she would share her husband's body with Andy, and asked if I would allow her to guide her children through me. I said I would be honored to carry on her memory and gave her permission to channel me to be with her children and grand children. All of the sudden I realized that I had been channeling her spirit for the last three years. She had unfinished business with her family and I gave her the opportunity to do that by channeling me. During the last three years, she mended her husband's guilt for not being able to fix her depression and she healed the anger that her son had for giving up on life and leaving him and the grand kids. He didn't understand why she didn't fight harder to live.

I had a warm feeling come over me. I knew that by allowing her to channel me, her spirit was able to come back and bring her loved ones peace. By allowing her to use me until her deeds were done, I got the chance to go to the other side and spend some much needed time with

Andy. When her healing of hearts was over she no longer needed to be here so I was called back. It benefited us both. Spirit will never ask for something without giving something in return. Everything is balance!

I asked my spirit guides what to do now? I have a wonderful husband that loves me and I have Andy at my side. The guides told me that nothing changed. I love my husband with all my heart and his wife's spirit is at his side. Once again everything is balanced.

Since then the family seems to be more peaceful. I can see the difference it has made in their lives. It still amazes me how things work. Although I have no memory of my journey with Andy, I am grateful for the time with him.

An Unexpected trip

I N October, 2013, after a long day of doing readings, I was preparing for bed. Just another typical night, so I thought. I crawled into bed and kissed my husband goodnight. I said my prayers and surrounded myself in God's light just as I always have. But when I laid down to sleep I felt the presence of Andy's spirit with me. He told me it was time to go. Before I could ask any questions I felt a pressure on my feet and I looked to the foot of the bed and saw Spirit holding my feet. Then I felt more Spirits in the room and looked to my side and saw an Angel and several more guides. Before I could say a word the process began. I could feel my entire spirit being pulled into my body.

I knew that feeling well and I was starting to get scared. I knew they were taking me to the other side. Once again a million questions flooded my mind. Would my children be okay? How would my husband handle the death of another wife? Would they feel me comfort them from Heaven? Then I thought of my daughter, would they feel my soul leave again? I asked God to comfort them. Then I looked to Andy and told him I was afraid. He just smiled and assured me it would be fine. I tried to panic but I couldn't. I was comforted through the whole process and somehow remained calm.

As my spirit energy was pulled into my body I felt heavy and could feel myself sinking into the bed. Then I began to spin. My eyes were moving faster and faster as if to follow what I was seeing. The spinning continued faster and faster, until I felt my soul release through the top of my head. When my soul left, my body felt light as a feather, almost as if it were floating on the bed. I could still feel Spirit holding my feet. Then I felt an energy starting to enter through my feet. It was coming in slowly and moving up through my legs. As the Spirit entered, my body started to become heavy again. Then all of the sudden I knew it was the spirit of my husband's first wife that was entering my body. When her soul was in completely, I could feel the spirits doing a process to ground her to my body. When it was complete, spirit opened my third eye and I saw my soul walking away with Andy. All the Spirits that helped the transition were now gone. The whole process took only minutes.

I laid there awake trying to fight sleep. Re-thinking everything that just happened, I had a million questions going through my head, but before I could ask, my eyes became very heavy and I could not fight it. I fell asleep. The next morning I woke and began questioning my guides right away. I had full memory of what had happened last night and I didn't know why. Was I gone for good? Did I die?

Why did I still feel like it was me? The spirit of my husband's first wife had walked into me before, but I was asleep and had no memory of it. Why did they keep me awake to experience the whole process? Once again the answers did not come. Every time I go through an experience like that it weakens me and I have a hard time connecting to my Guides. I stressed all day until my daughter got home from work. Once again I was hoping that maybe she could get some answers from her guides. I went to her house and asked her if she had a dream about me last night. Her jaw dropped and her eyes widened. She said she did not have a dream last night, but she dreamed the night before that I had died and passed into Heaven.

I told her what happened and asked if she could get her guides to answer. Just as she bowed her head to tune into her guides, I saw Andy and I's spirit come in behind her.

I was shocked and awed when I saw my spirit. I was so young and beautiful. I had channeled Spirit for years but never seen my own soul before. I told my daughter that Andy and I's Spirit was behind her and to ask Andy what was going on. Just then she lifted her head and said Andy assured her that everything is fine and their spirits began to pull away. The toughest lesson for me through the years is that my inquisitive mind does not always get answers when I want them. I have just trusted God and waited until Spirit was ready to reveal the answers.

The next day I needed to refresh my memory of the walk in process. I needed to know if there was anything in the book about a partial walk in. I knew that it was not a complete walk in because my soul was still aware as if a part of me was still here. So I referred back to my books. The book was written in 1974 and only covered a full walk in process and it said that it was permanent. The new walk in remained until the physical death of the body. I knew there was something more. I realized that there was nothing new on the subject and I would have to gain my strength back before I could consult my Guides for my answers.

Later that day I talked to a friend. She had taken my classes a few years ago and had become good in communicating with her guides. I told her what happened and she said that I went away to learn something to benefit my gift. She felt that I would be much stronger when I returned. She felt sure that I was coming back.

The next day I felt strong enough to meditate, and I was hoping for answers. When I felt connected I asked who was guiding me in Andy's absence. One by one, the Spirits all lined up in front of me. First my dad, I cried when I saw him. Dad had not been around me much and it always made me emotional when I felt his spirit. Then, the grandmother that raised me, my other grandmother that was the minister and then my Aunt. They all gave me time to thank them as they were showing themselves. Then my vision focused upward and Jesus stepped forward, followed by Mother Mary, Saint Germain and Arch angel Michael. I was so grateful for the vision they had given me and I felt very comforted by it. Then they stepped back and the vision was over.

I had asked several times over the next few day and my guides once again did not give me any answers. I have always had an inquisitive mind and wanted to know everything. My guides and teachers on the other side have grown used to my never ending questions, but once again, I knew I needed to trust God and be patient.

Five days later during meditation, my dad's spirit came to me and said that I was almost done. I still had questions and my dad said that everything would be revealed when I got back. The next day I was feeling extremely weak. As if something had drained all the energy out of me. I prayed for strength and my dad came to me again and said I would be back soon. I went in to lay down but I could not sleep. The chapters of my first book started flashing through my head. I asked if they wanted me to try to publish it again and was told NO. But the chapters continued to flash in my head. If finally became clear to me that my Guides wanted me to write a new book about only my experiences with them.

Recalling all my near death experiences, my experiences with them and everything they have taught me through meditation and readings.

Later that night I still felt very weak and turned in for the night. As I laid there I felt the presence of my guides in the room. Once again I had a weird feeling and could feel someone holding my feet down. I wondered if my soul was returning. Just as I had that thought I started to feel dizzy and started to spin again. This time it was not so aggressive. I could feel myself whirling and I just closed my eyes and let it happen. I could feel the temporary soul leave my body and was thanking her for watching over my body in my absence. Just as she pulled out, I once again felt a soul energy entering through my feet. This time it was a peaceful and familiar feeling. As the soul was entering my body I started to get visions. They were beautiful visions of gleaming white marble buildings, gorgeous floral landscapes and deep blue oceans and the feeling of an incredible love filled my body. I knew I was back from somewhere beyond and this time I was bringing memories of my journey back with me, as if I had taken pictures of my vacation. When my soul transition was complete, I could once again feel the Spirits working to seal my soul to my physical body. I somehow felt the urge to look down at my body and as I looked I saw a beautiful white light radiating from my entire body. I knew that I had once again, been to the place called Heaven.

I slept peacefully that night knowing that my soul was back. In the morning I could not wait to start writing my book. I had such excitement and as I began to type, the words and memories started to fill my head. My guides took me back to my first book and I found myself deleting a lot of my life as a child. What I went through as a child is not important. I have already released those memories and was healing from it. It is important for you to know that during those horrific experiences, my Invisible friends; (Guides and Angels) had been there through all of it, guiding me with love and support.

Messages From Spirit

D EATH:
My Spirit Guides wanted me to share my near death experiences with you and the beautiful things I experienced during them. They want you to know that we, as physical beings, are afraid of the unknown. As a child, my life experiences taught me to fear everything! Each time death came to me I was so comforted during the process, that it became a beautiful thing to me. Death is not the end of life. It is merely another form of existence. Through my years of working with light beings (guides), they have let me experience the feeling of the soul releasing from the body. The spinning process I have described helps us to raise our vibration to the spirit level. Spirit tells me they are all around us, but we cannot see them because we are grounded by a slower vibration.

Take a fan for example; when it is not vibrating we can see the blades in its solid form, but when it is plugged in, it is vibrating at such a speed that the blade becomes invisible to the eye. Yet the blades are still there. Lets take another example; the humming bird.

When the bird is observed in a still position on a branch its full form is seen. Yet when the bird is in flight, the wings move with such force that they become invisible to the naked eye. Yet the wings are still there.

The body's vibration is no different. Our physical bodies are vibrating at a low speed to keep us grounded to the earth. But our soul has the knowledge and ability to speed up with enough force that it can eject our soul out of the body. The silver cord that keeps our souls connected to our body is intact until God himself cuts it at our time of death.

It serves as a bungee cord during our travels, stretching infinitely to whatever destination we will ourselves to go. Our guides and guardians are always with us and will guide our journeys and keep us protected. We will always return to our body. Fear is the only thing preventing us from experiencing all that is available to us. It is limitless.

When our souls release for the final time, in the event of death our physical minds have taught us to fear the unknown. However, that fear only lasts a moment until the light of God wraps us in his comfort. At that time our soul will begin to vibrate at the same higher speed as our loved ones, allowing us to see and communicate with them. We are never alone at the time of passing. The light comforts us as we feel God's love wrap our body calling us home. We are drawn to it naturally.

Hell:

My guides tell me that Hell is not a place where the Devil lives. Nor it is filled with demons and monsters. It is merely a state of mind. We are God's children and he has taught us right from wrong. We were sent here to love and have compassion for each other. While we are here on earth our souls record all of our deeds. When we have loved and done good things, our souls are drawn back to our father with pride and accomplishment. However, when we have done bad deeds, and we have not asked the father for forgiveness, we punish ourselves by going to a lowest level. This is the hell state of mind. Our souls are obedient and will feel ashamed and unable to face our father with our deeds. If we have placed our self in the corner upon our return. our Father will council us and helps us to make amends for our deeds. We are given a choice. We can either comfort them from the other side until they no longer feel the pain we have caused or until that person has forgiven us, then we can release our soul from the deed and return to a higher level. If the deeds we committed are so horrible that they cannot be comforted, we can choose to return and try to do better. God loves us and has taught us to be obedient. God loves us unconditionally and does not punish us. We choose our own punishment.

Our lesson here on earth, is to find forgiveness for those who have hurt us and to move on. Forgiving them releases their soul from pain and frees you of hatred or anger toward that person. If we choose to never forgive, that karma may follow us into another life and we may not be forgiven for one of our acts. (Do unto others)

Grief:

This is an emotion that we feel when a loved one has gone home. The pain can be so severe that our soul feels the impact. My guides tell me that the pain we feel is unnecessary. It is a form of punishment for ourselves for not finding our faith in God. If we had the faith, we would not grieve because they are only a minute away in our mind and we can travel to see them through meditation anytime we wanted to.

My guides tell me that we don't grieve for the soul that has left, we grieve for the loss of the physical body. That part of our need for material things. Something we can see and touch. They tell me that if we could set our senses higher than what meets the physical eye, we could overcome this senseless grief.

We should rejoice when our loved ones go home. Be grateful for the time we had with them and the precious memories we have of them. The love and memories we share together are what keeps us connected to them in Heaven. Example; we are born to learn. First from our parents and then from school. While we are at school we make friends, form close bonds and help each other through the lessons. When we have learned our lessons we graduate and get to go home. We do not grieve for them when they graduate, we celebrate their life of learning and throw a party for their accomplishments. Even though we won't see them in school anymore, they still continue to guide us and help us through our lessons until we reach graduation, and they are there to celebrate with us when we get home.

Meditation;

We become so involved in our physical lives and the need to collect material things here on earth that we lose track of our purpose here. Our purpose is to love and be loved. Meditation helps us to raise our vibration and connect to the purest source of Love.

It calms our inner being and allows us passage to our loved ones and God on the other side. Connecting to the divine can calm our frustrations and give us guidance in our daily lives. Without it, life becomes chaotic and unbearable. By letting go of your fears your soul automatically takes you to that peaceful place you came from. As I said before, your soul automatically knows the way home. During meditation you may see a loved one or a spirit teacher or even a guide. Just let your mind take you on the journey.

Gratitude and love is the best feelings you can relay during this state of mind. When you are grateful for what you have been already given, then the father will give you more to be grateful for. Love is the ultimate emotion. By sending out love during meditation it will ripple all over the world and to all your loved ones and God. Remember that the feelings you send out during this heightened state of mind is more powerful. Our energy is crucial in this world, because everything is energy and it can be felt by all. If we would all send out love during meditation it would ripple around the world and be felt by every living being. We can change the world with our thoughts and emotions. We are constantly sending out thoughts and emotions all the time but the state of meditation heightens it. With this world being in such turmoil it is important that we all send love, peace and harmony into the world during meditation. It will make a difference.

Finding a loved one is easy during meditation. Just think of that person you want to see and try to envision their face in your mind. Think of all the love you have for them until your heart fills with the love, and then call to them. This works for guides as well. They are always with you. If you ask they will show themselves. Just trust what you see with your mind.

Guides;

Guides are the souls that we have assigned to ourselves before we came here. They are usually someone that we trust from a previous life. The guides we choose are an important part of our success in this lifetime. It is there job to keep us on task and help us to complete all that we have written for ourselves in this lifetime. The tasks we accomplish will help us to rise to a higher level in Heaven. Our guides are so in tune with every aspect of our being and there guidance flows through our minds as our own thoughts. A main guide is the one assigned to you from birth through death. Other guides will come and go as you need them. They all have a teaching purpose for different lessons we learn. Example; if you decided to be a fireman in this life, than a soul on the other side that has been a fireman in a previous life will come to guide you, etc. If you have been betrayed and had your heart broken and you decide to never love again, a guide will be sent to teach you how to trust and find love again. Remember, we are here to learn and if we choose to shut down after an experience, we are loosing precious learning time. It is our guide's job to keep us moving forward and to teach us. Everything we go through in this life is teaching us something.

Loved ones can become our guides as well if they choose. But in order to do so, they must take the time to read and study what we have written for ourselves so that they can guide us to get it done. This could take a lot of time depending on what we have written. I remember when Andy passed to the other side. I questioned why it took him 16 years to find me. He explained that he needed to go through his life review and then worked to study my records so that he could guide me. Remember that there is no time on the other side and what seems days or years to us is merely moments for them.

Heaven:

I could go on and on about this subject, but there have been enough books written about this subject and it can be anything you create it to be in your mind. There has even been movies about it; in "What Dreams May Come" I thought Robin Williams played a great part in what we can expect when we get there. I can only witness to what I have experienced in the previous chapters. I do know that if you have truly been to Heaven, there are no human words to describe the experiences or feelings.

My guides tell me there are many levels and depending on how many lives we have had, how much we have accomplished and the deeds we have done determines which level our souls are on. Each level of accomplishment brings us closer to God. My experiences in Heaven are indescribable, because every time I return from there my mind is erased. My guides tell me that if we could truly remember the experience in Heaven, we would not want to be here on earth. That is why our soul's memory is blocked when we come here. My guides also tell me that the moment we die everything becomes known to us again, our memories and all of the love and lessons from all life times are restored.

When we die our spirit sheds our physical body. We leave sickness and pain behind with the old body, which is nothing more that the vehicle we get around in. The body is also what keeps us grounded to this earth. There is no longer a need for it once we pass. When we leave our bodies, our spirit is revealed. It is perfect and beautiful in every way. Our spirit bodies do not hunger, tire or want for anything. What the spirit does not shed is personality or love. When our soul leaves this plane it takes all the love with it and carries it until you are together again. The love is what keeps you connected to the ones left behind. It is the doorway to visiting them again.

The personality is the makeup of the soul. It is the very essence of who they are. Every time a soul comes through in a reading, their personality is the first validation. If they were loud and loved to laugh, or if they were shy and spoke softly. That's the way they will come through in the reading. If they were a practical joker and life of a party, they will show it in the reading. They see everything here. From the birth of new babies to the things we are struggling with. They see us, feel us and hear us. They don't miss a thing trust me.

Material things do not go with us, we have no way to carry it. Think of it as having a house fire, when the fire breaks out there are only moments to think. The first thing you take is yourself and your loved ones. You do not have time to gather your material things and pack them up. They are lost in the fire and you have to rebuild them.

It is the same way in Heaven. You had to leave all your belongings behind. But you took the love with you and you can reconnect with your loved ones with that. As far as the material things go, well, you have to rebuild them. In Heaven you create everything with your mind. You think of it and what you want it to look like and it is there. It's that easy. The bible tells us that in Heaven, there are many mansions. You create the home for you and your loved ones. If a family member gets there before you and you don't like there creation, you can remodel it your way or build your own. You will never run out of space.

Traveling on the other side is as simple of thinking where you want to go and your there. Spirit travels at the speed of thought. Just think of a loved one and you are beside them.

If you always wanted to go to Hawaii and never got to go, just think of it and you are there. Its limitless in Heaven.

Communication:

Communication in heaven is nothing more than to think of what you want them to know and they hear you. It is all done by telepathy. When spirit comes to me in a reading their mouths do not move, yet I can hear them just fine because they are putting their thoughts in my head. This works great for foreign spirits, If I don't know there language, no problem. They transmit their thoughts to my brain and I automatically translate it. When spirit communicates with us they have to use the knowledge that is already in our head. So the more you have knowledge of the better. That is why learning is so important. But don't sweat if you didn't finish school. The information will come through in a way you can understand it. I often laugh with my guides as to why I was chose to be the medium cause their isn't much up there. I'm just a plain and simple kind of girl. My guides just laugh and say you don't need a college education to be smart.

Changes we need to make:

I asked my guides how to change the world and make it better and this is there answer:

Love: God's greatest gift to us is Love. The most important thing in this lifetime is to take time to love! So many people are focused on their jobs and how much money they make to buy material things. How big your house is, what kind of car you drive, or how much money you have in the bank will not matter in Heaven because you can't take it with you. The only thing you can take when the time comes is love and memories! The love you give now will be given 100x over in Heaven. Love is our ticket back to earth to be with our loved ones. Every time a loved one thinks about you in Heaven, you will feel that love magnified and you will be drawn to them. When we love one another in this world, that love will fill the earth and emanate to Heaven. Think of how it would feel 100x more.

Acceptance: Every single soul on this earth is here on there own journey. Journeys are as vast as the Heavens. We may not always agree with someone else's choices or what they decide to do with their lives but it is their choice. Everyone has Spirit guides watching over them to make sure they accomplish there deeds in this life. If they make mistakes it is part of their souls lessons to learn and grow. You need to accept that you cannot change someone else's path. The only thing you have the power to change is yourself!

Stop the Judgment: If you judge people in a negative way here on earth, then you will be judged negativity on the other side. God had revealed many things to me over the years through prayer and through my readings. Look back on the reading I did for a woman and her lover in Spirit. So much love came through in that reading that it brought tears to my eyes. God revealed that he is love and his greatest gift to us is to love and be loved. Who are we to judge who someone chooses to love? Twice I revealed how our judgment affects others. Do you want there suicide to be on your conscience when you get to Heaven? Think about it!

If we are at peace with the world now, then we will be at peace in heaven. There is only one way to be at peace here and that is to stop feeding into the negativity on the news and in our society, and practice sending love and peace through meditation. Do good deeds for others. Smile at someone and brighten their day. You don't know what they are going through at home or the struggles they face. If you make fun of someone with a mental disorder, chances are that soul is paying off karma for judging someone in a past life. Do you want to be paying the same price in the next life?

Be compassionate: Do and say everything with love and you can never do wrong. Follow your heart and let it guide you. Put yourself in someone else's shoes and you will see the journey they have had to endure. Compassion is Love.

Stop bullying: Every human being is energy and the energy we put into words and actions can hurt or damage someone's spirit. Time after time I have seen the souls on the other side that have taken their own life because of the emotional pain that was inflected upon them by another. There is so much senseless suicide. When a child is feeling that much pain, they choose to take themselves home to feel the love and embrace of God.

They are not punished by their act of suicide; rather they are rewarded for sacrificing their life to make a change in the laws.

Stop the religious war: Who are we to say what religion is the right one? There is only one God and hundreds of religions. We are usually taught the religion that our parents follow, but does that mean that particular religion will feel right to us? The average person will seek several different churches during a lifetime and maybe even switch there religion completely. They will seek until they find the one that feels right to them.

Every person on this earth is on their own journey, and each journey is different. We cannot inflict our beliefs upon them nor can we change their free will. It is their personal journey.

Greed: This is the mountain of all evil in this world. It is the need to possess something, whether it is money, material things or power. People feel empowered by it. Money is not the root to evil; it is a necessity for our survival. But when we become focused on having more, without being grateful for what we already have, then it becomes greed. If God has blessed you with abundance, he is testing you to see the good you will do with it. Do good deeds to help someone. Remember that all that you give will come back 4x fold. If not in this life, it will come in the next.

Creating Our Heaven Now

M Y SPIRIT GUIDES have taught me that everything
we do in this life affects the outcome of our
heaven. The more people we love and touch in some
way will send us love back on the other side. Everything
in heaven is magnified 100x over, good or bad! Think
about it for a minute. The people we give love to in this
life will think about us when we have passed. The love
they have for us will be felt in heaven 100x more. The
gratitude for the good deeds we have done for them will
be felt 100x more, and if we send out loving energy to
the universe in this life time it magnifies the love we will
feel in Heaven 100 x.

The bible states that thou will be done on earth as it
is in Heaven. I never really thought of it this way until I
started working with my Spirit Guides. It really makes
sense now. Imagine how many thoughts and decisions
you will change knowing this! The deeds you do, the
love you give, and the sacrifices you make will all be
rewarded and felt 100x. Think about that the next time

you send out something into the universe, the ripple effect it will have and how it will affect your heaven.

Everything in Heaven is balanced and so should it be on earth. What I mean by this is, when you get something you give something in return. Value does not come into play here. If someone gives you a gift of value, but all you have to give is your love or gratitude, it is balanced because you gave something in return. The greatest gifts we can give are love and gratitude. When you love someone here on earth, that love is returned here and in Heaven 100x.

Give of yourself freely. Spent some time with loved ones and make new memories, for that will follow you to Heaven. The more people you love here on earth, the more love you will receive on the other side 100x times over. Example: If you volunteer two hours of your time at a big brothers club to help some boys. That was only two hours of your time. No big deal right? Wrong. Let's say that in those two hours, you talked to and mentored 10 boys that needed to be helped. Those 10 boys will remember how you touched their lives for many years to come and every time they feel grateful for the difference you made in their lives, you will feel there love and gratitude in Heaven. Every good deed we do here on earth will follow us to Heaven.

Love is what we thrive on in Heaven. The more love you give now, the more you will feel in heaven. Think of it as a rechargeable battery: If you plug it in to charge for 8 hours, it will be energized for 800 hours (100x longer). Now think of how many hours you have spent loving someone here on earth, Magnify that number by 100. That's how long you will feel there love on the other side. Have you loved enough to keep your Heaven going? Now let's think about those good deeds you done for people. Every time that person thinks about your deed with gratitude it charges your battery up. How many times they think of that deed will depend on how much your deed touched there life. Bigger deeds will give you a bigger charge.

Now let's say that one of your deeds was paying for someone's much needed medicine. Not only will you be rewarded with gratitude for that deed, but the medicine helped them to live longer, so there are many more years that they will remember what you did for them. Now let's think of it the other way. You're a big executive at a pharmacy. You set the prices on the medicine marking it up to make a 90% profit. Your greed has just caused 100's of people to die because they could not afford the much needed medicine. Not only will you feel the sadness of the souls that died, but you will feel the anger of the family members that are left behind grieving. What energy do you want it feel in Heaven? I'm glad I am not a pharmacy and that's all I am saying about that.

Do not attach yourself to material things on this earth for they will parish in time. But the love you have for a house or a boat will be carried over in heaven. I am talking about our ability to create things with our mind. As I shared previously in my cross over story, my uncle really loved fishing. When he got to the other side, he was able to re-create his boat and his favorite lake. He was still doing what he loved. If you really love your house, don't cling to it here in the physical life. You will be able to re-create it in heaven. The point I am trying to make is that when you die and your soul leaves the body, you will go into the light, unless you dwell here because you are attached to material things. As I have said, our souls are on automatic pilot and know the way home, but we can delay that process by clinging to this physical life or material things.

I have seen it in readings. Some souls cling to their loved ones here because they fear letting go and never seeing them again. The truth is, if they let themselves go into the light, they will be cleansed of all negative and will be able to visit their loved ones any time they want and the speed of thought. Other souls cling to material things and will dwell on this earth until they learn to let go. If only they had known ahead of time that they can rebuild it in heaven. So much wasted time holding onto something out of fear of losing it.

Preparing for Heaven now can save you precious time on the other side. The more you learn to do here the faster you will progress on the other side. There is no time on the other side, so learning how to do things there could take a lot longer than to accomplish it here on earth. Communication is one of the examples. If we learn to communicate with our minds (telepathy) here, we can begin talking to our loved ones as soon as we pass, instead of taking months to learn it on the other side. Communication is easy, have you ever thought of someone and the phone rings and it is them? Well that's because you were sending your thought to them. Or if you were wishing that your spouse would take you out to dinner so you didn't have to cook, and he comes home and tells you he is taking you out. People that share the same thoughts don't have to be your soul mate. It merely means that they are on the same wave length as you.

We also communicate with our emotions. If a spirit comes through in a reading and I feel their love, I can relay that to the client. I feel all emotions in the readings, love, remorse, regret, etc. Spirit learns how to send their feelings as well. People tell me all the time that they can feel their loved ones with them. The love they are feeling, is what keeps them connected to us. You can do this now, example: when you go to a wedding, you can feel the love in the room and the happiness makes you cry. Or if you walk in a room where someone has just had an argument, you feel the tension. We all emanate emotions, in this life and in heaven.

Travel is another one, when we want to go somewhere we think of where we want to go and get in the car and drive, but on the other side, we think of where we want to go and we will ourselves to go there through thought. As fast as we think of it, we're there.

Some people can already do this, as I described earlier in the chapters. I thought about my mom and let my soul travel there. I saw what she was wearing, where she was sitting and what she was watching on TV. It is possible to learn this right now. We just need to let ourselves go. We do it all the time when we day dream or dream when we sleep. Like I said, our souls are on automatic pilot. They already know what to do.

Our souls are drawn to heaven every night while we sleep. While our body is at rest, our Soul ventures to the other side to visit our loved ones. That's why dream visits are so common. Sometimes we remember the visit and sometimes we don't. Our minds choose to forget or shrug things off as a dream because it cannot comprehend what it has just seen.

Meditation is important because it teaches us how to change our vibration level. All spirits vibrate at a different level according to what level there soul is on in heaven. We need to learn this in order to visit our loved ones on different levels. For example; we can communicate to other people here on earth because they are on the same level as us, but to communicate with a soul that passed, we need to dial up our energy to communicate with them. It's like fine tuning a radio station. Keep adjusting until you hear them and then hold that position. This can also be done by visualizing during meditation. Imagine yourself floating on air. Now let yourself rise up a few feet and hold your position, if you don't feel anything, then let yourself rise again. You will know when you have connected.

Fear is what we are taught from the time of birth. Constantly being told to be careful, or don't do that or you will hurt yourself etc. We are taught all our life to fear. The key to your soul's progress is to overcome all the fear we have been taught in life and give our souls the freedom to explore. If Christopher Columbus would have listened to everyone telling him not to explore because the world was flat and he would fall to his doom, he never would have discovered a whole new world. Which by the way, now that there is proof it exists, we have all tried to find it and some have even moved to the new world because we liked it. Just saying!

Fear holds our souls progress down. When we give into our God given abilities it can show us some amazing things. We are all interested in our history. And some have even built or investigated our family trees. Where we came from, who are loved ones are, and we are always looking back at what we have accomplished in our past. Why stop at this life? Why not get the whole picture? Our lives are infinite and our soul records everything. There is so much more to know and explore.

Don't fear it, just let your soul go exploring. If death is what you're afraid of then, you are wasting your time.

Death is part of life. It's inevitable and there is nothing you can do to change it. Do you really think you can bargain with God? When it's your time and God comes for you, you won't be able to talk your way out of it. It will just happen. Just remember, the fear only lasts a moment until you are surrounded in the light that comforts you and calls you home. Your soul knows the journey. You have done it many times before, and you will do it again. Our existence is infinite. So what do you really have to lose?

You just might find that beautiful place of existence. The place where love and peace exists. Where there is no hatred or judgment. Wouldn't it be wonderful if we could discover that place of love and bring back a little piece of it each time we visit. Think about how it would change the world here if everyone brought back a little piece of unconditional love. That is my wish for the entire world. Instead of hatred, negativity and drama, just turn the other cheek and walk away from it. Don't feed into it, just choose to ignore it. The more you feed into it, the more it will consume you. The choice is yours. You decide what you want in your life, here and on the other side called Heaven.

Spirit Visitations

S PIRITS CAN VISIT us in numerous ways. They can
visit us in their normal spirit body, which is clear and
almost invisible to the eye. The easiest way to see them
in this form is to look at something across the room. It
will appear clear to the eye without interference. But
when a spirit form moves in between you and what you
are looking at it will become slightly blurry. Almost like
looking at the heat waves rising from the hood of your
car on a hot day.

When spirit is conserving there energy, they become
the form of an orb, (a ball of light). They generally do
this when they are traveling from one place to another.
Orbs have sometimes been seen with the naked eye, but
most orbs have been caught in photographs. If they are
moving fast the orb will look like a streak of light. We
can also see them with our peripheral vision. Usually as
a moving shadow, or a flash of light, almost like a flash
bulb going off beside us. But when we look to see it, it
is gone.

Spirits can materialize and appear to be standing in the room with us. This is rare because they have to lower their vibration to become a solid form and it takes a lot of their energy to do this. If this does happen it will only last a few seconds.

Spirits will often move things, make our phones ring, cause our lights to flicker, or change the channel on our TV etc. These minor things take the least of their energy and spirits are very good at manipulating electrical devises because they are energy themselves.

It is not their intention to scare us! They merely want to give us a sign that they are with us. I have often had clients ask why there loved ones are not giving them signs, but when I ask if it would freak them out if it happened they say; heck yes! Well that's your answer; they don't want to scare you.

Spirit can also use their energy to manipulate animals, birds and insects. They can get them to come to you to help send there sign. I had a client tell me that just before her dad passed, he told her he would come to her in the form of a butterfly. Shortly after his passing she saw butterflies everywhere. That was his sign to her. The signs that spirit give us will somehow bring us peace and comfort. Most of all, it keep reminding us that they are with us. This reminds me of the saying; "Their not gone until they are forgotten". They constantly keep reminding us that they haven't left us.

Another way Spirit can visit us is through channeling. Generally this is done through a skilled medium or channel er. However, as I described before you don't always need a medium to talk to your loved ones. Andy was perfectly capable of channeling through a perfect stranger in the club that night; just to spend a few moments with me. The point that I am trying to make here is to always be aware of our surroundings. You never know when a loved one will take the opportunity to be with us.

I have seen this happen many times, particularly when a spouse passes over. When you have finished grieving and decide to move on with your life and find a new partner. Your loved one's spirit will channel through the new lover. My clients have actually felt the difference in their touch, or their new love will say the exact same thing there spouse used to say.

I also explained the walk in process that Andy went through to be with me. In the books and information I have studied, it says that the walk in process is final until death of the physical soul. However, through my personal experiences, I have learned that not all walk-ins are permanent. When Andy walked into my husband he showed me that it was not permanent. He only stayed long enough to bring us together and fall in love. That is called a temporary walk in. Andy now continues to channel my husband when he needs time with me in the physical. Just as my husband's wife channels me to be with him and the family.

Temporary walk-ins will transition only long enough to accomplish a task and then they step out. When this happens, the physical soul will go to the holding place until the task it is done and then they will return to the body with the change already in place. When a spirit walks in, it leaves behind their imprint. Example: When Andy walked into my husband, the incredible love he feels for me was left imprinted in the physical body. When my husband's soul returned he felt that love for me. This is another way that God brings us together when it is meant to be.

Channeling is different. Every time I channel a spirit during a reading, I can feel the love or emotions they have for the client. But channeling is a process of the spirits energy overlapping with mine, not coming into me. Example: every living being is energy. Our aura is the energy around our body. Like a bubble of energy. When I do a reading, I push my energy out, (making my bubble bigger) the spirits energy then steps into mine. When this happens, I can feel their energy as if it were my own. When the spirit steps out of my energy, I can no longer feel them. During a reading, I can see and feel the spirits in the room, but they stand back, meaning they are present for the reading, but they don't have a message.

Spirits can channel anyone at any time, including you, by merely stepping into your aura they can transpose there energy onto you. Example: you are sitting in your chair at home watching TV. All of the sudden, you become emotional and start thinking about a loved one. This is a visit!

When the loved one steps into your aura, your soul feels them and that will trigger your memory of them and your emotions will kick in. The same goes for negative emotions. When a negative spirit walks into your aura you will start to feel anger or start to have bad thoughts. This could be a spirit that you have bad memories with. His/her energy can trigger bad thoughts. When this happens, just refuse the energy and tell it to leave you in the name of Jesus or whatever higher power you believe in.

God's Law:

There are laws on the other side, and the first and most important law is, if a Spirit is unwelcome, they cannot stay! If you tell them to leave they must leave or they will be banished.

On the other hand, good spirits and guides are always around you. If you feel a spirit presence around you, and you're not sure if it's good or bad, then cast them out! If it's bad they must leave. If they are good, they merely back up. Guides and guardians do not leave because they are there to protect and guide you.

It is important to be aware of your feelings or moods at all times. When you start to feel anger or negative, evaluate your feeling. If something happened to cause you to be angry then it is your feeling and you have the choice to continue feeling that anger or not. But if you are angry and have no reason to be, then that emotion has been imposed upon you from either entering your aura or thought projection. You can remove it by telling it to leave.

Thought projection is when a spirit telepathically thinks of you and sends you a thought or emotion. Our souls are made to automatically pick up on these vibrations. So again, make sure it is your thought and not coming from someone else.

It is important that you know energy and projection does not have to come from a soul in Spirit. It can come from a physical person as well. As I have said, our souls automatically pick up on energy, we are born with it. That's why it is important to choose your company wisely. If we are around negative people our souls will absorb it and it will become part of our emotions. Have you ever been in a good mood and visited someone that is negative and always complaining about something. When you leave that persons energy you feel like crap? That is a good sign that you have absorbed their energy. We will talk about that in the next chapter.

What is Energy?

I could go on and on about this topic. I have been empathic since the age of four. This is the sense of feel. Not only have I felt my invisible friends since a young age, but I could also feel people's emotions around me. I feel energy, and everything is made of it.

By learning to work with your energy, you can open some amazing doors.

Energy is the essence of our being. We use it for everything and don't even realize we're doing it. We use energy while we're having a conversation. Every word we speak carries some kind of emotion that is using up our energy. Example: If we have an argument with someone. Every word that comes out of our mouth is filled with emotion. If that argument lasts long enough we become exhausted and finally quit. The same goes with trying to prove your point about something, if the person receiving the information is blocking your opinion it is exhausting you. When you have a good conversation and the flow is back and forth, it is balanced and the energy will continue.

Love is energy also. When you are giving love to someone, you are sending good energy and when that love is returned, it is balanced! We talked about balance earlier and how important it is to have balance in everything. When our energies are balanced we never feel depleted. But if you are giving love to someone and that love is not being returned, it is one sided and you will become exhausted. That is a good way to tell if your relationship is working or not. One sided relationships never work because you will eventually become depleted and walk away.

We are constantly using energy. In person, on the phone or even in our thoughts. My guides have taught me that it is important to always be positive. When we are sending out positive energy, the universe recognizes it and will send it back 4x fold, but negative energy works the same way. Again, we have the choice of what kind of energy we emit.

Just be aware of the ripple effect it will have. One person's energy can make a difference, but if everyone would change their thoughts and send energy as a group, we can really make a difference.

When our energy becomes depleted, there are many ways we can recharge ourselves. We can do nothing and our souls will start to recharge over time. Again, our souls are automatic and know what to do. We can meditate and raise our vibration to connect to the universal flow of energy, or we can go outside and walk. By grounding ourselves to the earth we can pull from earth source. That's why it is so important to put out good loving energy. The energy we put out replenished the source of flow. The same source we will be pulling from when we become depleted, so you want it to be a good source.

Energy is amazing and when you realize how valuable it is, we become more aware of what we are sending out. Our hands become a big part of how we send or receive energy. We send and receive with the palms of our hands. Everything from healing energy to love and resistance. Example: when I am sick, I open my hands and receive the healing energy God is sending me. When someone is talking to me negatively I hold my hand out in a stop position. Some people do this when they are saying "Talk to the hand". However, what they are really doing is blocking the flow of energy coming to them. The people sending the negative energy will feel the block and back off because if it is not being received, the energy will bounce off and go back to them. They will become uncomfortable and back off.

Thoughts are energy and when we think of someone with negativity or hatred, that energy will travel to them and they will feel it. Some call this voodoo, but the reality is, we are merely transmitting energy with our thoughts. Voodoo or energy only works if the person receiving it is willing to except that energy. Again you have the choice. If you feel the discomfort of the negative energy, refuse it by casting it out of your aura.

Love energy is the same. If a person thinks of you with loving thoughts, you can either receive and reciprocate that feeling or ignore it. A good example of this is being in a room and someone is looking at you with interest from across the room. Your soul will feel the energy, thus drawing you to the source of the energy. If you look at the source and don't like what you see, your soul will automatically stop the reception, thus giving the person sending it an uncomfortable feeling and they will stop sending the energy of interest. If you like what you see, your soul will automatically return the energy of interest.

This is important for those looking for love. If a long lasting love is what you are looking for, your energy is putting that out there and anyone else looking for that will receive it, being drawn to you. Lust works the same way, so be careful what energy you are putting out there.

The old saying is: "You have to love yourself before anyone else will love you is true"!

My guides have taught me that when you love yourself and are feeling good about yourself and feeling confident, that is sending out firm, positive energy and people will pick up on it. However, is you have low self esteem and tell yourself that no one will ever love you; you are sending out that kind of energy and people that receive that energy will have the same feeling of doubt about being with you. So it is very important to pay attention to the type of energy you are emitting. If you are already in a happy relationship and are content, your soul will not put out energy of interest. If a person goes against the content feeling and approaches you anyway, they will be rejected and their feelings are hurt. That's why it is important to trust your gut, (The energy your feeling). If you go against your feelings there is a price to pay. Thus rejection or worse. If you are being approached a lot and it is not what you want, it is important to double check the energy you are sending out. Are you really happy?

Energy can be amazing once you discover how to use it. Our energy is very powerful. This is an exercise I love to teach: On a sunny day, go outside and pick out a small puffy cloud, not too big or it will use too much energy, and focus all your energy on the cloud with the intent to dissolve it. After a few moments, the cloud will begin to fade until it has disappeared completely. If you did it right, you should be saying WOW right about now. We send energy with our intention as well. That's why it's important to not have thoughts of bringing harm to someone. If we wish ill intent upon someone our energy may cause something bad to happen to that person. That deed will then be recorded by your soul and you will have to deal with that karma or let it impact your life review when we get to the other side. Either way it won't be good.

When you're thinking of someone you are sending thought energy, so don't be surprised if they show up at your door or call you on the phone. You can invite a loved one in spirit to visit you in the same way. Just think about them and the energy will find them and draw them to you. Energy travels fast. If they don t come or call, it is not because they don't feel your energy. It usually means that they are busy and there by free will, they chose not to respond to your invitation. Trust me they always feel it. Sometimes I will begin to miss Andy and the energy of that thought is automatically sent. I know that he is always in tune to my energy, so if he does not come, I know he is busy at the moment. Even if he is busy, he acknowledges my energy by sending me a poke in the side. He is really good at poking me. I asked him one day how he does that? His response was to think of poking me in the side and sending that thought. His energy is so strong that when I receive his thought, it will actually poke me in the side. Kind of amazing when you think about it.

Sending hugs to heaven works the same way. Think of the person you want to hug. Envision yourself hugging them and send that energy with intention. Your loved one in Heaven will literally get the hug you sent and may even send one back. Sending thought energy with intention is incredible. Just think, you'll never be lonely for a hug from someone in Heaven again.

Now that I have taught you what energy can do, I need to teach you of the importance of forgiveness. We talked about that in Creating Your Heaven chapter. You should have a better understanding of how important it is to forgive. Our thoughts carry emotion. If you are continually sending negative thoughts to the one that hurt you in heaven, you are torturing that soul. That becomes a source of karma for you. Forgiveness helps you to heal from the pain and gradually stops you from thinking about them. When you have finally let it go, you will no longer transmit your emotions. This will bring peace to both of you and become balanced. We are all one with God and when we stop hurting someone else, we stop hurting ourselves in the process.

Energy is powerful when it is combined with visualization as well. A good example of this is creating something for yourself. God is a creator and we are born in his image, making all of us little creators. The ability is already within us. When you want something bad enough you can create it by thinking about what you want and visualizing yourself as already having it. By doing this, you are drawing that to you. The more you put energy into that thought, the more you are creating it.

God gave us five senses coming into this world. See, Feel, Hear, Touch and Smell. Those senses are a needed for creation. When we use all our senses and combine it with our energy we can create. The more we use our senses, the stronger they become. By heightening our five senses, we develop the sixth sense, "The Knowing"! When you have developed the Knowing, you will discover your God given power and all things are possible.

God has always said; "Seek and you shall find".

There is a hidden sixth sense born within you. It is the gift of Knowing. The ultimate gift that will connect you to God, "The source of unconditional Love and Truth".

Your soul knows!

Acknowledgements

I would like to thank Vicki DeKam for her time
and tireless dedication in editing this book.

And also
My wonderful Husband for his
incredible love and patience.

About the Author

DENISE BATTEES WAS born and raised in Portage, Michigan. Where she spent the majority of her life. She married her husband Vernon Battees in 2010 and now resides with her loving husband in Lawton, Michigan.

Denise started her own business, "Messages From Heaven" in the year 2000 in hopes of teaching people about Heaven and Death. She continues to channel her loving Spirit Guides to give healing messages from loved ones on the other side.

If you would like to know more about her work, or are interested in her work books, please visit her web site: www.deniseroot.com or join her on facebook.